Art Quilts at play

IGNITE YOUR INNER ARTIST—EXPERIMENT WITH SURFACE DESIGN TECHNIQUES

JANE DÁVILA & ELIN WATERSTON

C&T PUBLISHING

Text copyright © 2009 by Jane Dávila and Elin Waterston

Artwork copyright © 2009 by C&T Publishing, Inc.

Publisher: Amy Marson

Creative Director: Gailen Runge

Acquisitions Editor: Jan Grigsby

Editor: Deb Rowden

Technical Editors: Nanette Zeller and Rebekah Genz

Copyeditor/Proofreader: Wordfirm Inc.

Design Director/Cover & Book Designer: Christina D. Jarumay

Production Coordinator: Tim Manibusan and Matthew Allen

Photography by Christina Carty-Francis, Diane Pedersen, and Luke Mulks of C&T Publishing, Inc., unless otherwise noted

Published by C&T Publishing, Inc., P.O. Box 1456, Lafayette, CA 94549

Library of Congress Cataloging-in-Publication Data

Dávila, Jane.

Art quilts at play / Jane Dávila and Elin Waterston.

p. cm.

Includes index.

Summary: "Art Quilts at Play was developed for artists of all levels who want to try new things, experiment with art materials and artistic styles, and expand their visual repertoire"-- Provided by publisher.

ISBN 978-1-57120-530-8 (paper trade : alk. paper)

1. Quilting. 2. Textile painting. 3. Art quilts. I. Waterston, Elin II. Title.

TT835.W37593 2009

746.46'041--dc22

2008020481

Printed in China

10 9 8 7 6 5 4 3 2 1

Clima, by Jane Dávila

DEDICATION

for Carlos, besos . . . Jane

for Louisa, cha cha cha . . . Elin

ACKNOWLEDGMENTS

Jane and Elin would like to thank . . .

Jan Grigsby, Deb Rowden, Amy Marson, Christina Jarumay, Tim Manibusan, Casey Dukes, Matt Allen, Teresa Stroin, Nanette Zeller, Rebekah Genz, Diane Pedersen, Claire Oehler and the staff of the Country Quilter, and the collaborating and student artists who made this project possible.

Jane would like to thank . . .

. . . her family—especially Carlos and Samantha for their unflagging support and encouragement, as well as their good-humored tolerance for dusty corners, half-finished sentences, and late-night deadlines.

Elin would like to thank . . .

. . . David for putting up with her and letting her do whatever she wants for the past twenty years; Lexi for advice and inspiration; Loren Anderson and the staff of the Katonah Art Center; and Ryan, Jeff, and Rhett for the music.

Nancy, by Elin Waterston

Contents

Imprima: Pescado,
by Jane Dávila

INTRODUCTION

This book was developed for artists of all levels who want to try new things, experiment with art materials and artistic styles, and expand their visual repertoire. We've called it *Art Quilts at Play* for two reasons. First is the surface design element—literally playing with, exploring, and experimenting with surface design methods and techniques and art materials and products. Second is the metaphorical playing—getting involved with groups, collaborating, and setting up trades and challenges.

The first section of the book focuses on fabric design and creation and special effects for fiber and mixed media art. The second section suggests ways to connect with other artists—whether in cyberspace or real space. It also provides collaborative project ideas. Both sections encourage you, the artist, to have fun. Our hope is that you will give yourself permission to play, to experiment, to push through creative blocks by moving beyond your usual methods, and not to worry about the outcome while learning new things.

We've included galleries with examples of products from both areas of play—art made by students from our surface design classes and art from colleagues who we invited to collaborate with us on various projects.

el crisantemo, by Jane Dávila

HOW TO USE THIS BOOK

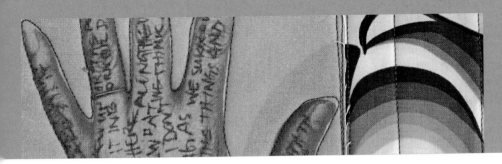

Often, the best way to master techniques is to play and experiment. This book includes instructions for a variety of surface design techniques and special effects, but many of these instructions should be considered suggestions rather than rules. Although certain rules apply for some techniques, you should feel free to try your own thing and do a little rule bending. We are presenting a few ways to use some materials and techniques, but these are by no means the only ways to use them.

We encourage you to try all the techniques and materials presented in this book. Some will appeal to you, some won't. That's OK, because nobody likes everything, and not every technique is appropriate for every project. We feel it's important

for you to get a basic understanding of as many techniques as possible. Even if you don't have an immediate use for everything, you'll have the knowledge to pull from when a project comes up that could benefit from something described here.

We also encourage you to participate in collaborative art projects—whether it's an Artist Trading Card swap, a more complex project, or something you develop and host yourself. Any participation in projects with other artists can inspire and challenge you and help you find your place in the art world.

Most of all, we encourage you to play with artistic techniques and explore materials that are new (or new to you) and keep pushing yourself to learn.

Supplies

Although many of the surface design techniques covered in this book use common materials, each will require some specific supplies and equipment. In general, the better your supplies and equipment, the better the outcome of your project. That said, it's not necessary to break the bank. Start out with small amounts of supplies, try different brands of paints and dyes, buy one screen-printing screen or lino block, until you find your favorite materials and methods. We recommend using either fabric paint or acrylic paint for many techniques. Fabric paint usually requires heat setting to render it permanent. Acrylic paint will cure in 2–4 days and not require further setting.

Motif created with Shiva Paintstiks

Motif created by painting with Jacquard water-based resist and fabric paints

Motif created with painted fusible web

Although we have included in the instructions our best personal knowledge regarding the washability of each material or technique, the art and projects that we make are not meant to be washed. If a product's permanence and washability is important to you and your project, we recommend that you do some research with the manufacturer.

BASIC SUPPLIES

- prepared-for-dyeing (PFD) cotton fabric and an assortment of other commercially dyed and printed fabrics of various fiber content

- drawing pencils and sketchpad

- various paintbrushes

- iron and ironing board

- parchment paper

- scissors for fabric

- scissors for paper

- freezer paper

- low-tack paper tape

- protected work surface

OPTIONAL (BUT HELPFUL) SUPPLIES

- appliqué pressing sheet

- digital camera

- scanner

- computer

- color ink-jet printer

- image-editing software

- toaster oven (for shrink film and polymer clay)

- lightbox

Safety

Some of the techniques in this book involve materials that should be used with care, so please take any necessary safety precautions. Work in a well-ventilated area, wear rubber gloves, and use a mask or respirator when working with materials with strong fumes or unpleasant odors or anything that can be airborne. And, of course, take extra care if you have any special health issues, such as allergies or respiratory ailments. Carefully follow all manufacturer instructions for use and storage of materials. Keep all toxic materials and sharp tools away from children and animals. Play it safe and err on the side of caution.

Many of the supplies (paints, dyes, and inks) are permanent, so always protect your workspace and dress for a mess!

Our Obligatory Note on Copyright

When in doubt, ask for permission to use an image or photograph.

Never assume that an image is not copyrighted; always assume that it is.

Just because an image is old or the creator is deceased doesn't mean the copyright has expired. If the heirs or the rightful owners of the copyright have renewed it, it is protected.

Changing an image by at least 10 percent is not a copyright loophole. Copyright law protects against derivative work.

An excellent source for definitive information regarding copyright law is www.copyright.gov.

Finally, remember that a big part of being an artist is finding your personal style. Don't depend on others' art to create your own.

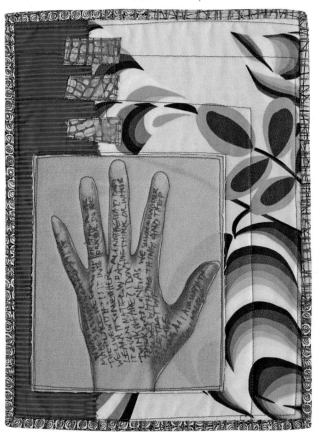

Cheiromancy: fate, by Elin Waterston

GLOSSARY

haiku, by Jane Dávila

antique—to add the appearance of age

arashi—a shibori technique in which fabric is wrapped around a pole before dyeing

baren—a small, flat pad used to impress a print

batching—a curing process in which newly dyed fabric or thread is kept at room temperature for 24–48 hours

brayer—a hand roller used to spread ink or paint

burnish—to rub, smooth, or polish

chop—an artist's seal traditionally used as a kind of signature in the Far East

compression dyeing—a method of dyeing in which some form of mechanical resist is used to create patterned areas of dyed and undyed fabric

cure—the hardening process of liquid or wet material that aids a material's permanency

discharging—the process of removing color from fabric

distress—to give the appearance of prior heavy use

extender—a medium added to paint to increase its volume without changing its color

ground color—the base color of paper or fabric used for printing

gutta—a thick, rubbery resist that is removed from fabric by dry-cleaning

gyotaku—a traditional Japanese relief print made from an actual fish

hand—the drape or softness of fabric

immersion dyeing—the process of dyeing fabric by immersing it into a tub or basin filled with dye solution

inclusion—element that is enclosed within another material

ink—to cover a surface to be printed with paint or ink

marbling—the process of mottling or streaking with color in imitation of marble

mask—a pattern used to shield selected areas of a surface

mesh—the fabric stretched across a screen-printing frame

migration—the movement of one color of paint or dye from one area of fabric to another (usually undesired)

motif—a dominant or repeating form, shape, or figure

off-registration—improper placement of a screen, causing the colors of a print to be incorrectly aligned

open time—paint's drying time

organic—an irregular shape or a shape found in nature

overdye—to immerse a dyed fabric in a second dye bath or to dye a hand or commercially printed fabric to alter the original colors

overspray—sprayed paint or ink that misses the surface to be coated

pigment—coloring material

prepared-for-dyeing (PFD) fabric—fabric that has been prepared for dyeing, so no finishes remain that would interfere with dyeing or painting

priming—the process of making preliminary test prints for the purpose of coating or sealing the surface of a printing block or plate, allowing for a better final print

proof—a test print made before a final print

pulling—removing a mould and deckle from a vat of paper pulp when making handmade paper; the action that creates the sheet of paper

relief—the three-dimensional projection of areas from a surface

resist—a medium that prevents a coloring agent from adhering to fabric or that stops the flow of a medium from one area to another

retarder—an additive that slows the drying time of paint

scouring—prewashing fabric to remove any dirt or sizing that would prevent the fabric from accepting dye

screen—a hardwood frame stretched with a very fine mesh fabric

sealant—a material used to coat or seal a surface

shibori dyeing—a traditional Japanese shape-resist dyeing method

squeegee—a tool with a flexible rubber side used to force pigment through the mesh of a screen frame

stencil—a sheet of material with a design cut into it so when a coloring agent is forced through the open area, the design is recreated on the surface beneath it

trapping—a method of creating stencils, used for multicolor screen printing, in a manner that allows the colors to overlap

trapunto—a quilting technique achieved by rows of stitching and padding to form an embossed, raised design

viscosity—the measure of fluidity

wash—a thin, translucent layer of pigment

CHAPTER ONE:

FABRIC CREATION

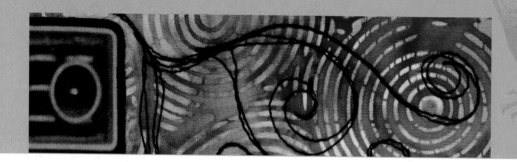

"The whole idea of making art is to be open, to be generous, and absorb the viewer and absorb yourself, to let them go into it. I have to go into all those places in order to make it work." —Frank Stella

play—(v.) to amuse oneself in a way characteristic of children; to occupy oneself in a diversion or recreation (from Middle English *pleye*: to leap for joy, dance, rejoice)

Mixing Color

Before embarking on surface design techniques, which involve ink, paint, or dye, it's important to have a basic understanding of color theory, including the relationships between colors and how to mix them.

The first step is to learn the color wheel. The traditional color wheel is based on the primary colors red, yellow, and blue—the three colors that cannot be made by combining other colors. All other colors are created from these primary colors. There is another school of thought about the color wheel—the CMY color model, in which the primary colors are cyan, magenta, and yellow. These colors, along with black (the K in CMYK), are the colors most often used in printing. Some people find the CMYK, or CMY, color model to be a more accurate

way of mixing color. In either case, it is difficult to mix paint, ink, and dye to achieve accurate colors if you do not start with accurate primaries. Therefore, it is important to test pigments (in small amounts) to make sure your starting primaries yield the appropriate hues. The more you practice, the better you get at mixing color.

> **⊙ NOTE**
>
> *In this book, we use the traditional red-yellow-blue color wheel. However, it is important for you to decide which school of thought works best for you for each project.*

THE LANGUAGE OF COLOR

hue—the name of a color

value—the lightness or darkness of a hue

shade—comparative darkness of a hue

tint—a light value of a hue; one with less than maximum saturation

primary colors—the three hues—red, blue, and yellow—that are equidistant from one another on the color wheel and that cannot be made from any other colors

secondary colors—the three hues—orange, violet, and green—that are equidistant from one another on the color wheel and that are each made by combining two primary colors

tertiary colors—the six colors—red-orange, yellow-orange, red-violet, blue-violet, yellow-green, and blue-green—that are between the primaries and secondaries on the color wheel and that are made by combining a primary and a secondary color

analogous colors—colors that are next to each other on the color wheel, usually not more than three or four colors (red, red-orange and orange; or red, red-orange, orange and yellow-orange)

complementary colors—colors that are opposite each other on the color wheel and that together contain all three primary colors: red and green (green = blue + yellow); blue and orange (orange = red + yellow); yellow and violet (violet = blue + red)

WARM AND COOL COLORS

Although color temperature is actually a characteristic of light, pigment colors are often described as having a temperature. Reds, oranges, and yellows, for example, are considered to be warm, and violets, blues, and greens are cool. To make this even more confusing, there can be warm blues and cool reds. A color's temperature is also relative; the appearance of some colors can seem warmer or cooler, depending on the colors that surround them.

Most color mixing problems occur when the primaries are skewed to be either too cool or too warm. For instance, if you are mixing paint to create a violet hue (which tends to be the hardest to create), you mix blue and red. If either the blue or the red is too warm (with a high yellow content), your resulting violet will be brown and muddy. Because yellow and violet are complementary colors, they neutralize each other, causing the color to go brownish. Certain brands of inks and paint have primary colors that are accurate primaries and mix well. You might find that you have to do a lot of testing (and buy lots of paint) before finding the most accurate colors.

Take it all with a grain of salt—everything depends on the accuracy of the primaries. But color theory is just that—a theory. If you understand the concept, you can make the jump from theory to practice.

Supplies

- pencil
- palette
- paintbrushes
- acrylic paints—primary blue, primary yellow, primary red, black, and white
- watercolor paper
- paper towels or rags
- small container of water

CREATING AN RYB COLOR WHEEL

1. Draw a large circle on a piece of watercolor paper.

2. Draw a small circle inside the first circle.

3. Divide the outer ring into 12 even sections.

4. Label the sections according to the chart.

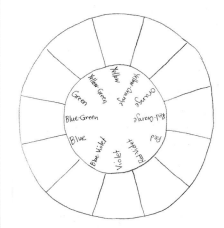

Wheel divided into 12 sections and labeled with primary, secondary, and tertiary colors

5. On a palette, squeeze out a small amount of each primary paint (red, yellow, and blue).

6. Paint the primary colors in the coordinating sections on the color wheel.

> **NOTE**
> *Wash your brushes thoroughly and replace your water before moving to the next color. Any residual color in your brush or water will compromise the purity of the hues you're mixing.*

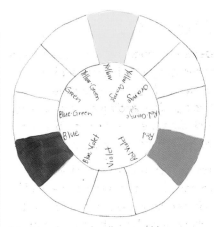

Primary colors: red, yellow, and blue

7. Mix the secondary color orange (red + yellow) and paint it in the appropriate section.

> **NOTE**
> *Keep in mind that some colors are stronger than others. When mixing colors, you will not necessarily use equal parts of each color.*

Create orange by mixing yellow and red.

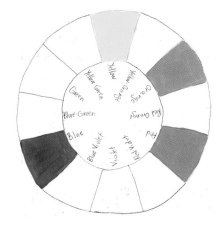

Paint the orange in the appropriate section of the color wheel.

✳ **TIP**

Use a second piece of watercolor paper as a tester sheet and test colors before painting them in your chart. It sometimes takes several attempts to get the appropriate hue.

8. Mix the other two secondary colors—green (blue + yellow) and violet (blue + red)—and paint them in the appropriate sections.

☉ **NOTE**

It's tempting to jump to tertiary colors before finishing the secondary colors (like mixing yellow-orange while you're mixing orange). Don't do it, because you'll gain a better understanding of color mixing if you follow the order.

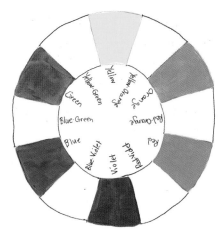

Paint the remaining two secondary colors.

9. Mix the tertiary colors one at a time: yellow-green (yellow + green), yellow-orange (yellow + orange), red-orange (red + orange), red-violet (red + violet), blue-violet (blue + violet), and blue-green (blue + green). Paint them in the appropriate sections

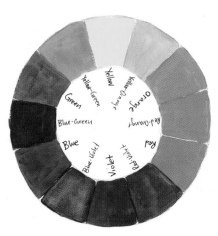

Completed color wheel, with primary, secondary, and tertiary colors

NEUTRALIZING COLORS

Many people add black to a color to make it darker, but this can cause a shift in the hue and is not always the appropriate way to darken a color. Adding a color's complement (opposite it on the color wheel) can darken and dull it or take the edge off it. Varying the proportions of primaries and their complements creates new colors, including rich browns.

1. On a piece of watercolor paper, draw a grid of 1″ × 1″ squares, 7 across by 3 down.

2. Label the squares to represent the colors you are mixing. The first row is red; then red plus a small amount of green, red plus a medium amount of green, red and green mixed to create a neutral brown, green plus a medium amount of red, green plus a small amount of red, and finally green:

top row: R (red); R + 1G; R + 2G; N; G + 2R; G + 1R; G (green)

middle row: Y (yellow); Y + 1V; Y + 2V; N; V + 2Y; V + 1Y; V (violet)

bottom row: B (blue); B + 1O; B + 2O; N; O + 2B; O + 1B; O (orange)

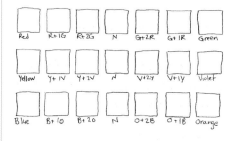

☉ **NOTE**

This is not an exact formula. Some colors are stronger than others, so you do not always add equal parts of paints or dyes to create new colors. Paints and dyes vary brand to brand as well, so experiment and test colors before starting a project.

3. Put red and green paint on a palette (mix blue and yellow to make the green).

4. Paint the first square in the first row red.

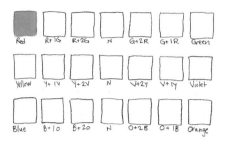

5. Mix a very small amount of green into the red and paint the second square in the first row this new color.

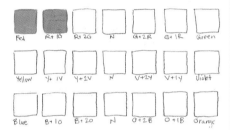

Red plus a small amount of green

6. Add a bit more green to the red-green mixture and paint it in the third square of the first row.

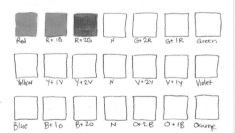

Red plus more green

7. Go to the other end of the row and paint the last square in the first row green.

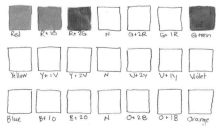

Paint the last square in the row green.

8. Mix a small amount of red into the green paint (get fresh paint as needed) and paint this color in the sixth square of the first row.

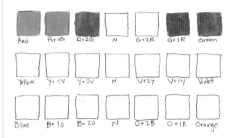

Green plus a small amount of red

9. Mix a bit more red to the green-red mixture and paint it in the fifth square of the first row.

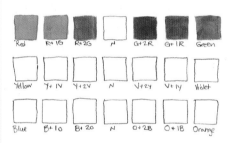

Green plus more red

10. Mix green and red together to create a neutral brown and paint it in the middle square in the top row. Remember that you won't necessarily use equal parts of each color.

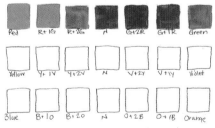

Green and red mixed together to create brown

> ⊙ **NOTE**
>
> *Black is a very strong color. Use small amounts of black when mixing it with other colors.*

11. Repeat this process in the second row, using yellow and violet paint.

12. Repeat the process again in the third row, using blue and orange paint.

GRAYSCALE

1. On a piece of watercolor paper, draw a row of seven 1″ × 1″ squares.

2. Squeeze a small amount of white and black paint onto a palette.

3. Paint the first square in the row white.

4. Add a very small amount of black to the white to make light gray and paint it in the second square.

5. Add another small amount of black to the light-gray mixture and paint it in the third square.

6. Paint the last square black.

7. Add a small amount of white to the black to make a dark gray and paint it in the sixth square.

8. Add a small amount of white to the dark-gray mixture and paint it in the fifth square.

9. Mix black and white to make a middle gray and paint it in the middle square.

Completed grayscale

SHADES AND TINTS

Adding black to a color creates shades; adding white creates tints.

1. On a piece of watercolor paper, draw a row of seven 1″ × 1″ squares.

2. Paint the middle square a primary color—red, yellow, or blue.

Primary blue

3. Mix a small amount of white into the primary to lighten it. Paint this color in the third square (to the left of the middle).

4. Add more white and paint it in the second square.

5. Add even more white and paint it in the first square.

Primary blue with three tints

6. Mix a very small amount of black into the primary color (get fresh paint as needed). Paint this color in the fifth square (to the right of the middle).

7. Add more black and paint it in the sixth square.

8. Add more black and paint it in the last square.

Completed tint/shade scale

> ◎ **NOTE**
>
> *Adding white to a color causes a shift in hue. This can be counter balanced by adding a small amount of an adjacent color on the color wheel.*

> ◎ **NOTE**
>
> *Remember that unless the paint is completely opaque, the ground color of the support (i.e., the fabric or paper) affects the color of paint.*

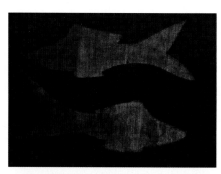

Red-orange paint screen printed on black, turquoise, and light blue fabric

Fabric Dyeing

Dyes form a molecular bond with fabric (the dye molecules chemically react with the fiber molecules). This bond does not change the texture or hand of fabric as paint can. Procion dyes are fiber-reactive dyes for use on natural fibers (specifically cotton, rayon, linen), which must be set by steaming or batching. Several brands of dyes are available, in numerous colors in both powder and liquid form.

Many variables are involved in fabric dyeing. White fabric results in the purest color reproduction. When dyeing off-white or other colored fabric, keep in mind that the original color of the fabric will affect the end results, so know your color wheel and be sure to make a test swatch. The amount of color in your dye bath will also affect the resulting color of the fabric, as will the amount of time the fabric remains in the bath and the hardness or softness of the water.

It's important to do tests and understand that results will be somewhat unpredictable. Remember, the color of the fabric when wet is two or three shades darker than it will be when dry. Soda ash and noniodized salt can be added to the dye bath to aid the chemical reaction of the dye. Dye stocks can be stored for several weeks in the refrigerator; however, once soda ash has been added, the dye begins to react and will only last about eight hours.

BASIC HAND DYEING

Basic single-color bath dyeing can be done in a bucket, basin, or washing machine. Prewash the fabric to remove sizing. Dampen the fabric evenly, fan fold it into the dye bath, and agitate frequently to create even, allover color. To achieve an uneven, mottled look, crumple dry fabric and then immerse it in the dye bath.

OVERDYEING

Interesting effects can be achieved by overdyeing commercially dyed or printed fabric. Know the color wheel and use it to your advantage. Overdyeing fabric with its complementary color will take the edge off the color and make it more neutral. With white-on-white fabrics, the ink will act as a resist, which means it will not reach the same amount of saturation as the fabric. Therefore, it will either be a paler shade or will remain white.

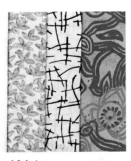

Commercially printed fabric

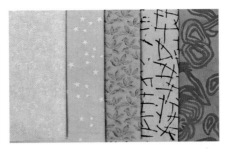

Commercially printed fabric overdyed with turquoise dye

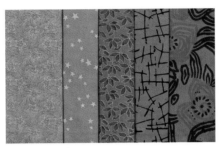

Commercially printed fabric overdyed with red-orange dye

SHIBORI-STYLE COMPRESSION DYEING

Compression dyeing is a shape-resist dyeing technique for creating patterns on fabric in which the fabric is compressed before it is placed in an immersion dye bath. The compression prevents the dye from penetrating the resisted areas, forming patterns of dyed and undyed fabric. Shibori is an ancient Japanese practice that encompasses a wide variety of compression dyeing techniques in which a design is created by wrapping, binding, stitching, clamping, or twisting fabric before it is placed in a dye bath. This method can result in anything from simple textural patterns to highly complex designs. Though traditional shibori dyeing is rarely practiced any more, modern compression dyeing methods have been developed to make shibori-like dyeing simpler and more accessible.

There are endless ways to stitch, fold, tie, twist, clamp, and manipulate fabric for compression dyeing, each creating a unique pattern. As with any surface design technique, experimentation is the key.

Fabric twisted and bound with rubber bands

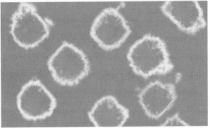

Fabric wrapped around glass stones and bound with rubber bands

ARASHI (POLE WRAP) SHIBORI DYEING

Supplies

- PVC pipe
- ¹/₂ yard prewashed cotton fabric
- ball of twine
- dye solution
- noniodized salt or soda ash (optional)
- bucket or tub
- garbage bags
- plastic bins (like dish pans or kitty litter bins)
- rubber gloves
- paper towels and sponges (It's messy!)
- rubber bands

1. Wrap a ¹/₂ yard of scoured or prewashed fabric around a length (about 20˝) of PVC pipe.

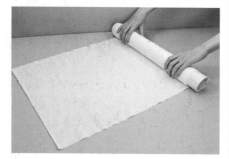

Carefully roll fabric on the pipe.

2. Wrap the end of the twine tightly around the fabric at one end of the pipe and tie it in a knot.

3. Continue wrapping the twine around the fabric, spiraling up to the top of the pipe. Tie off the twine and secure it in place with a knot.

✳ TIP

You might find it helpful to work with a teammate, with one person turning the pipe while the other person wraps.

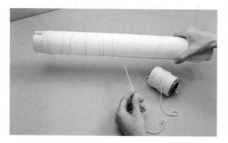

Keep twine fairly tight on the pipe.

4. Working from the bottom up, scrunch the fabric, a little bit at a time, down to the end of the pipe.

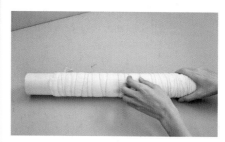

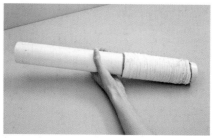

Scrunch the fabric down to one end of the pipe.

✳ TIP

Place a rubber band at each end of the scrunched fabric to help prevent slipping.

5. Prepare a dye solution in a bucket, following the instructions specific to the brand of dye you're using. If desired, add noniodized salt or soda ash to the dye solution.

6. Immerse the pipe into a bucket containing the dye solution, making sure all the fabric is covered by the solution.

Immerse fabric-wrapped pipe into the dye bath.

7. Leave the fabric in the dye bath, stirring occasionally, until the desired color is reached. (Remember, it will be two to three shades lighter when dry than it is wet.)

▣ NOTE

In general, the longer the fabric is in the dye bath, the deeper the resulting color. However, there is a saturation point at which no more color can be absorbed. The fabric on the outside of the pipe is usually darker than the other layers of fabric.

8. When the dyeing process is complete, remove the pipe from the dye bath, letting the excess dye drip back into the bucket.

9. Place the fabric-wrapped pipe in a plastic garbage bag and put it into the plastic bin for batching. Do not remove the fabric from the pipe or untie the twine. Leave the pipe in the plastic bag for 24–48 hours to allow the dye to cure.

10. When the batching is complete, remove the fabric-wrapped pipe from the bag and run cold water over the fabric to remove excess dye solution.

11. Cut the twine and unwrap the fabric.

12. Rinse the fabric in cold water until the water runs clear.

13. Machine wash fabric in cold water with a mild detergent.

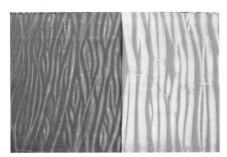

PVC pipe–style (arashi) shibori-dyed fabrics

FOLDED FABRIC COMPRESSION DYEING

Folding fabric is another way of creating a shaped resist. Folded fabric is dipped into a dye solution, or dye is directly applied to folded fabric with a paintbrush or squeeze bottle. This method creates textural or geometric patterns of color.

Supplies

- prewashed cotton or PFD cotton fabric—fat quarters (approx. 18″ × 22″)
- 3 or 4 shallow, wide-mouth containers
- dye solution in 3 or 4 colors
- resealable bags (sandwich or quart size)
- rubber gloves
- protective covering (newsprint, plastic drop cloth, etc.)
- twine or rubber bands (optional)

> 🌀 **NOTE**
>
> *Folded fabric can be bound with twine or rubber bands.*

1. Accordion fold a fat quarter of fabric (in 4 or 6 folds) into a long strip.

> 🌀 **NOTE**
>
> *The more folds, the more intricate the resulting pattern will be.*

Accordion fold fabric into a long strip.

2. Fold in one end at a 45° angle and continue accordion folding until all the fabric is compressed into a triangle shape.

3. Press the folds to create crisp edges. Bind with twine or rubber bands if desired.

Accordion fold the fabric strip into a triangle.

4. On a protected work surface and wearing rubber gloves, prepare 3 shallow, wide-mouth containers of dye solution, each with a different color.

5. Dip one corner of folded fabric into a container of dye solution.

6. After a few seconds, remove the fabric and squeeze or let the excess dye drip back into the container.

7. Repeat Steps 5 and 6 with the second and third corners, using a different color of dye for each corner.

Dip the remaining corners in dye.

8. Place the folded fabric into a resealable bag and seal.

9. Allow the fabric to cure by leaving it in the bag at room temperature for at least 24 hours.

10. Unfold the fabric and rinse it in cold water until the water runs clear.

11. Hand wash the fabric in cold water and a mild detergent.

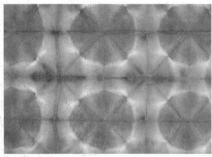

Folded and dyed fabric

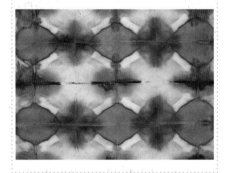
THREAD DYEING

Natural fiber threads and yarns can be hand dyed with either one color to match a hand-dyed fabric or with several colors to create a variegated thread.

Supplies

- heavy cotton thread (like sashiko thread) in hanks
- thread for tying (hand quilting or button thread)
- small containers of dye solution in several colors
- small foam brushes
- plastic cling wrap
- resealable bags (sandwich size)
- rubber gloves
- protective covering (newsprint, plastic drop cloth, etc.)
- glass or ceramic palette or paper plate

1. Using a heavy thread (or a small piece of the thread you're dyeing), tie off a hank of sashiko, or other heavy cotton thread, into about six sections.

2. Arrange the hank on a palette in a circle, so no areas of thread are touching.

Place tied thread on a palette.

3. Prepare your desired colors of dye according to the manufacturer's instructions in small containers.

4. With a foam brush, dab one color of dye solution onto one area of the hank. Allow the thread to absorb the color.

Apply first dye color to the thread by dabbing with a foam brush.

5. Repeat Step 4 with a different color for each tied-off section of thread, using a clean brush for each color.

Continue to dab colors to sections of thread.

6. Wrap the thread completely in plastic wrap to prevent migration of the dyes to unwanted areas.

7. Place the wrapped thread into a resealable bag and keep it at room temperature for at least 24 hours.

8. Rinse the thread in cold water, while still tied, until the water runs clear.

9. Allow the thread to dry.

10. Cut the ties and roll the thread into a ball or wind it onto a spool, if desired.

✳ TIP

To avoid tangles, don't manipulate the thread too much at any point during the dyeing or rinsing processes.

✸ TRY THIS

- *Fold fabric and hand or machine stitch patterns for immersion dyeing.*
- *Hand stitch and gather fabric before placing it in a dye bath.*
- *Wrap fabric diagonally on PVC pipe to create slanted lines.*
- *Dye textured yarns and threads.*
- *Experiment with yarns and threads that contain synthetic fibers (lighter shades will result).*
- *Wrap colored fabric on PVC pipe and immerse it in a diluted bleach solution for discharged arashi patterns.*

Simple Screen Printing

Partifish, **by Elin Waterston, quilt made using a multicolored screen print**

Screen printing is a form of stencil printing in which ink or paint is forced through a screen that has an impermeable area and an open design area. This method allows the pigment to be deposited onto fabric (or paper) in the unmasked areas only. Although many screen prints are made using either a light-sensitive photo emulsion or a drawing fluid and a screen filler to mask the design, it is also possible to use a plain paper stencil that will adhere to the screen after the first print pass.

Images and design elements can be screen printed on white or other solid-colored fabric, or they can be layered over hand-dyed or printed commercial fabric. Be sure to test ink and paint colors on fabric before printing.

Screen prints can be made using a single stencil with a single color, a single stencil with mixed colors, or multiple stencils with multiple colors. Single or multiple images or an overall pattern can also be screen printed.

Overall pattern screen printed onto fabric

When creating a multicolored print, layer each color using a separate stencil. Lighter-colored stencils can be cut slightly bigger than the actual size so that dark colors can overlap, eliminating unprinted areas of fabric. Working from the lightest to the darkest color will create trapping, which means dark colors will overlap light colors. Alternately, stencils can be cut to the exact size and pigment applied in terms of farthest to closest (starting with the background color and working toward the foreground). This method is less accurate and sometimes results in unprinted areas.

Even under the best of circumstances, screen printing isn't always an exact science. Sometimes registration is way off or the pigment is not evenly distributed. But don't discard off-registration prints; their imperfections and irregularities just add to the charm and give them personality.

Small quilt made using a print with improper registration

SCREEN AND FABRIC PREPARATION

To prepare the prestretched screen, wrap duct tape over all the edges of the wood frame, extending about $1/2$″ onto the mesh on the inside of the screen. Add more tape to the bottom of the screen, lining up the edges of the tape with the tape on the inside of the screen. Allow the tape to cure for 24 hours to prevent it from coming unstuck when printing. The tape will help waterproof the wood and will create a trough to hold any unused ink or paint after the print pass has been made. After the tape has cured, use a toothbrush or nailbrush to scrub the screen with cool water and soap or a household cleanser. Dry it thoroughly.

Prepare the screen by covering the frame with tape.

Prewash all fabric to remove sizing or finishes, which can prevent the pigment from adhering, or use a PFD fabric. It's best to use cotton or natural fabrics, because synthetic fibers won't accept the paint as well as natural fibers will.

When using screen-printing fabric inks or fabric paints, follow the manufacturer's directions for setting the color (most require ironing to heat set the colors) once the pigment is completely dry. Note that acrylic paints do not require heat setting.

Supplies

- stretched screen-printing frame (prepared as described above)

- squeegee, about $1/2$″ narrower than the screen's inside measurement

- fabric or acrylic paints or screen-printing fabric ink in squeeze bottles

- plain paper—drawing or white construction paper, a few inches larger than the screen

- X-acto knife

- cutting surface

- prewashed and pressed cotton fabric or PFD fabric

- masking tape

- paper towels and baby wipes

- nailbrush or toothbrush

- rubber gloves (if you don't like to get your hands dirty)

- protective covering (newsprint, plastic drop cloth, etc.)

- small jar or can

PAPER STENCIL: SINGLE COLOR

1. Create a design stencil. Draw a design on a piece of paper that is cut to the size of the screen's outer edge. Remember that the pigment will be blocked from the fabric wherever the paper is, so plan your design accordingly.

Create a design on drawing paper.

✳ **TIP**

Make a copy of your design so that you can cut out stencils and keep your original design. Cut out several stencils, in case you need backups while you're printing.

2. Use an X-acto knife to cut out your stencil. Keep both the positive and the negative areas of the stencil, so you can make prints using both the positive and negative images.

Carefully cut out the design.

Keep both the positive and negative stencils.

3. Lay out the prepared fabric on a smooth, protected surface, making sure there are no wrinkles or folds in the fabric. Tape it in place if desired.

4. Place the stencil on the mesh side of the screen (tape it to one end if needed).

Place the stencil onto the screen and tape in place.

5. Place the screen mesh side down onto the fabric.

6. Squeeze ink or paint along one end of the screen. You will learn from experience how much paint you'll need for each pass.

7. With one hand, hold the screen firmly in place on the fabric. With your other hand, hold the squeegee at an angle and carefully pull it across the screen, forcing the ink or paint through the mesh and leaving any excess ink or paint in the trough at the opposite end.

8. Scoop up any leftover pigment with the squeegee and pass it across the screen in the opposite direction.

9. Wipe off the squeegee with a paper towel or baby wipe and set it aside.

10. Carefully lift the frame, separating it from the fabric by hand if needed. Wipe away any excess ink or paint and set it aside, resting the frame on a small jar or can to prevent any ink or paint from getting onto your work surface.

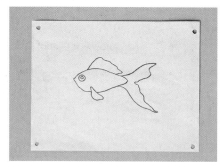

Original drawing of a two-color design

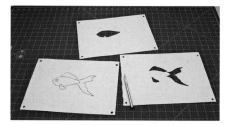

Cut stencils for each area of color.

2. Make a copy of each section of the stencil. Use an X-acto knife to cut out the area to be printed.

3. Mark each stencil with its coordinating pigment color.

4. Lay out the prepared fabric on a smooth, protected surface, making sure that there are no wrinkles or folds in the fabric. Tape the fabric in place.

5. Place the first stencil on the mesh side of the screen (tape it to one end if needed).

6. Place the screen mesh side down onto the fabric.

Finished leaf print (single stencil, single color) on fabric

 TIP

If you are doing a single print, clean the screen immediately, otherwise the ink or paint might dry and clog the mesh. Wash the screen with warm water, soap, and a nailbrush or toothbrush. Dry it with a rag or paper towel to prevent warping. Allow it to dry completely before using it again. If you are repeating the same image on other parts of the fabric, reposition the frame on a blank area and repeat the process in the desired areas. If you're printing the design on multiple pieces of fabric, have all the pieces taped in place on your work surface so they are ready to be printed. Work quickly and clean the screen as soon as you've finished the last pass.

PAPER STENCIL: MULTIPLE COLORS

1. Draw an original design on a piece of paper that is a few inches larger than your screen. The design should consist of 2 or more color sections. Determine which color each section will be.

◉ REGISTRATION NOTE

When printing a multicolored design, you can register your stencils to ensure that colors are in correct alignment with each other. In general, printing screens have registration pins on the base. Holes are punched in the paper to be printed so it can be placed on the pins, assuring the correct placement for each color run.

There is a simple (albeit, less accurate) way to do this when printing fabric. Draw your design on paper that is a little larger than your screen. Carefully stack the paper (one piece of paper for each color stencil you will need) and punch holes through all the layers close to one edge or in all four corners of the paper. (Be sure to allow a little room at the edge of your design for this.) Using these holes as a guide, make a stencil for each color pass by aligning each layer over the original drawing and tracing the area to be printed. Cover your work surface with newsprint and lay the fabric pieces on the newsprint, taping them in place if needed. Place the original drawing on the fabric in the desired position. With an indelible marker, color in the circles on the newsprint under each piece of your fabric or on the fabric itself. You can then use these dots to line up the screen for each color run.

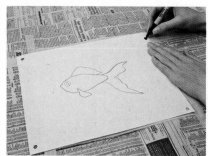

7. Squeeze ink or paint along the trough at one end of the screen.

8. With one hand, hold the screen firmly in place on the fabric. With your other hand, hold the squeegee at an angle and carefully pull it across the screen, forcing the ink or paint through the mesh and leaving any excess pigment in the trough at the opposite end.

9. Scoop up any leftover ink or paint and pass the squeegee across the screen in the opposite direction.

10. Wipe off the squeegee and set it aside.

11. Carefully lift the frame, separating it from the fabric by hand if needed.

The fish's body is made in the first pass.

12. Allow the first color to dry.

13. Repeat the process for each color (including background colors, if desired) until all sections have been printed.

The fins and tail are made in the second color pass.

✸ **TRY THIS**

Use more than one color of ink or paint and mix the colors in the screen to create a marbled effect.

Print made with a single stencil, mixing two paint colors in the frame.

Nature Printing

peixe, **by Jane Dávila**

Nature printing consists of using forms from nature in either direct or indirect printing. Natural objects such as leaves, fish, vegetables, fruit, and even the sun can be used to create unique fabric.

With the exception of sun printing, nature printing techniques can be done on most fabrics, from plain white to dark commercial prints.

SUN PRINTING

Sun printing, or heliographic imaging, is the ultimate organic painting experience. Nature itself becomes your collaborator in the creation of your fabric. Use a PFD fabric or a prewashed white or light-colored cotton fabric. The fabric is painted and then covered with an assortment of flat items. When the wet fabric is placed in the sun (or under a heat lamp), all the areas masked by the flat items leave a lighter imprint. Results will vary wildly, depending on light conditions, breezes or wind, the wetness of the fabric, the items chosen to mask the sun's rays, and the colors of paint used. The lack of control over the many variables is one of the charms of sun printing. Delight in the unexpected!

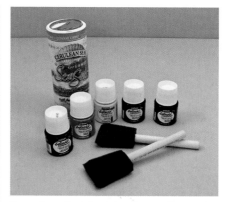

Setacolor paints, foam brushes, and sea salt used in sun printing

Supplies

- prewashed white cotton, or PFD fabric—fat quarters (approx. 18″ × 22″)
- Setacolor transparent paints
- 20″ × 30″ cardboard or foam core board
- plastic dropcloth cut to cover board
- 2 or 3 foam brushes
- spray bottle filled with water
- 2-cup plastic containers
- sea salt (optional, but fun)
- items to be used as masks— Natural items like leaves or flowers can be fresh or dry, but they must be thin and flat (press them in a book if necessary before using). Soft leaves work better than stiff leaves. Other ideas include designs cut from paper, thin wood cutouts, lace, cheesecloth, feathers, seashells, and starfish. You'll need enough masks to cover all of your fabric at the same time.

PROCEDURE

1. Mix 2 parts water with 1 part Setacolor paint in plastic containers.

❋ TIP

For pastel or lighter colors, mix 3 or 4 parts (or more) of water with 1 part paint.

2. Spread the fabric over plastic-covered cardboard or foam core board.

3. Spritz the fabric with water to dampen, keeping fabric very flat.

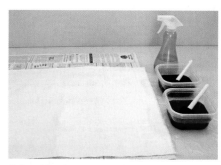

Colors blend more on wetter fabric and less on drier fabric.

4. Use long, smooth strokes of a foam brush to apply one or more colors of diluted paint.

The results are most effective with one to three vibrant colors.

5. Once the entire fabric is painted, quickly arrange your "mask" items onto the fabric. Tap the items so that they become saturated and the edges stick evenly and flatly to the fabric surface. If desired, toss a little sea salt onto the fabric. Sea salt creates spontaneous starburst patterns as it pulls the moisture out of the painted fabric.

The flatter the items, the crisper the impression they will make on the finished fabric.

✳ TIP

If the day is breezy, you can keep your mask items in place by laying a piece of fine tulle over the fabric before placing it in the sun. The resulting print will be slightly diffused. Make sure the tulle is larger than your fabric. Weight the edges of the tulle with pebbles, coins, or washers.

6. Place the board with the wet fabric in the sun (intense, early afternoon sun works best) or under a heat, halogen, or grow lamp for anywhere from 15–20 minutes to as long as an hour, depending on conditions. All the areas covered by the masks will be lighter than the areas exposed to the sun.

✳ TIP

Items that don't sit completely flat on the fabric will yield fuzzier, hazier images as compared with the crisp images formed by flat, well-stuck items. If you move your fabric before it is completely dry, make sure it stays flat. Crinkles or folds in the wet fabric will result in lighter areas.

The brighter the day, the crisper the images.

7. To check on the progress of your sun print, carefully lift one corner of one of your mask items.

8. Once you reach the desired effect, remove all the mask items, brush off any salt, and allow the fabric to dry completely. Heat set the colors by ironing the fabric for 2–3 minutes on a cotton setting. The fabric does not need to be rinsed. The colors are now permanent, and the fabric is washable.

Finished fabric sun printed with leaves

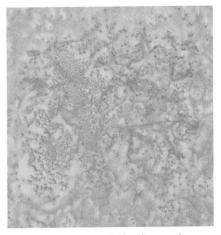

Finished fabric sun printed with sea salt

☀ TRY THIS

- *Custom masks can be created by cutting shapes out of plain paper.*
- *Overlap various items to suggest depth.*
- *Toss items on wet fabric for a fuzzier, casual look.*
- *Scrunch up your fabric while it's wet for a random light/dark effect.*

Fabric made by allowing it to dry while scrunched up.

NATURE OBJECT PRINTING

Many plant materials can be used for printing. In the direct printing method, the item is inked and then pressed to fabric to create an impression. By playing with materials, colors, fabric, and positioning, you can create a truly unique piece of fabric.

A variety of produce suitable for printing

A variety of leaves suitable for printing

LEAF PRINTING

1. Lay out the prepared fabric on a smooth, protected surface, making sure there are no wrinkles or folds in the fabric.

2. Place a leaf vein side up on some newsprint. Apply one or more colors of paint to the leaf, smoothing out your brush strokes and avoiding excess paint.

Don't forget to paint the stem.

3. Using your fingers or tweezers, carefully pick up the leaf and place it painted side down on the fabric.

Don't move the leaf once it has touched the fabric.

Supplies

- prewashed white or light to medium-colored cotton fabric or PFD fabric

- newsprint

- fabric or acrylic paint

- 1/2″–1″ paintbrushes or foam brushes

- parchment paper

- paper towels

- protective covering (newsprint, plastic drop cloth, etc.)

- tweezers (optional, but helpful)

- leaves: Avoid thick, fleshy leaves. Look for different sizes, types, patterns, and interesting edges. Durable, flat leaves with strong veins work best. Pick leaves fresh and refrigerate in plastic bags or press between damp paper towels.

- vegetables and fruit: Firm, fresh produce, such as apples, pears, onions, peppers, and cucumbers, work best, but many fruits and vegetables can be printed.

4. Cut a piece of parchment paper larger than your leaf and place it over the leaf. With one hand, hold the leaf or press down to prevent shifting. With the other hand, rub the leaf from the vein out.

Rub the edges and the stem. Avoid repeating areas to prevent blurry images.

5. Remove the parchment paper and leaf and discard the paper. A sturdy leaf can be used several times before it is unusable. A fragile leaf, such as a fern, may fall apart as it is removed from the first printing.

Leaf print on fabric

※ **TIP**

To create the illusion of depth, leave the first leaf in position and place another leaf over it, overlapping slightly. Continue adding leaves until you have reached the desired effect. Don't wait too long, as the paint will dry and the first leaves will stick and be difficult to remove.

※ **TRY THIS**

- *Use a small brush to blend several colors of paint on the same leaf.*
- *Print the leaves in clusters or overlapping patterns.*
- *After printing, add detail with colored pencils, paint, or fabric markers.*
- *Paint one leaf several times and reprint over a previous printing to add depth, being careful to maintain registration.*

Multiple leaves printed on the same fabric

PRINTING PRODUCE

1. Lay out the prepared fabric on a smooth, protected surface, making sure there are no wrinkles or folds in the fabric.

2. Slice produce to expose the inside. Place the cut side of the produce on paper towels to absorb excess moisture.

3. Apply one or more colors of paint to the object, smoothing out your brush strokes and avoiding excess paint.

Don't apply too much paint, as your prints will be indistinct.

4. Place the produce painted side down on fabric and press firmly.

Be careful not to shift or wiggle as you press to avoid blurring the print.

5. Remove the object and apply more paint to print again. Produce will last through a day's printing session—maybe even longer with refrigeration. If the surface becomes too clogged with paint and detail is becoming lost, cut off a thin slice to expose a fresh surface.

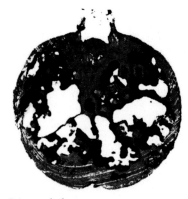

Finished fabric with onion print

 TRY THIS

Blend several colors of paint on one vegetable or fruit.

Print made from cucumbers

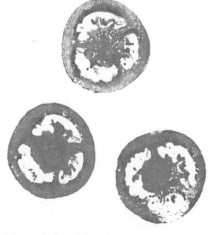

Print made from jalapeño peppers

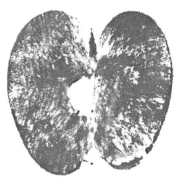

Print made from pomegranate

Print made from apple

Print made from kiwis

Print made from pear

FISH PRINTING

A variety of rubber replica fish

Printing fish, or gyotaku, is a traditional Japanese printing technique developed more than 100 years ago as a way for sports fishermen to record their catch. The traditional technique employs freshly caught fish. However, several companies now produce fish cast in rubber from actual fish. The resultant fish prints can be used as an integral part of an art quilt, or they can be cut apart with pieces incorporated into an original piece. The detail and life of the fish are truly caught in the printing.

Supplies

- prewashed, light-colored cotton fabric
- fabric or acrylic paint
- rubber gyotaku fish
- foam brayer
- inking tray, sheet of aluminum foil, or disposable plastic plate
- fine paintbrush
- newsprint
- paper towels

PROCEDURE

1. Prepare two work areas with newsprint. One will be the inking area and the other the printing area.

2. Place your fish on clean newsprint in the inking area.

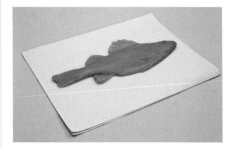

Make sure your fish is clean and dry before starting.

3. Squeeze a small amount of paint (1 or more colors) onto an ink tray, sheet of aluminum foil, or disposable plastic plate.

Start with a small amount of paint and add more as needed.

4. Evenly coat the brayer by rolling it in the paint. You can blend 2 or more colors by shifting the brayer slightly from side to side.

❋ TIP

Be careful not to blend multiple colors too much, as the colors will blur together and look muddy.

Two colors blended together will lend your fish a more naturalistic appearance.

5. Evenly cover the fish in paint by rolling the paint-covered brayer over it.

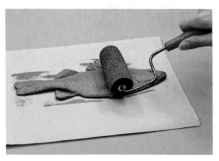

Roll along the top and sides.

6. Move the inked fish to a clean piece of newsprint (the printing area). Use a paper towel and your finger to carefully wipe the paint off the fish's eye.

Move the fish to a clean area.

The eye will be painted by hand later.

7. Determine the center of your fabric. Starting at one end, carefully lay the fabric over the inked fish. Use your fingers and palms to rub and press the fabric to the fish. Work into all areas, including the edges, fins, and tail. Be very careful not to shift the fabric.

8. After you have pressed and rubbed the entire fish, carefully peel up the fabric from one end to another and lay it aside to dry.

Try not to rub over the same area twice to prevent smudging.

Lift up the fabric slowly and evenly to reveal the completed print.

✳ TIP

Lightly scrub the fish with a nail brush and get into all of the nooks and crannies. Otherwise, you will have less definition the next time you print due to leftover dried paint. Try not to let the paint dry on your fish, as it will be hard to remove.

9. If you intend to print the fish again in the same color, move the fish back to the inking area onto a fresh piece of newsprint. If you intend to use a different color, wash the fish thoroughly and pat it dry with a paper towel.

10. After the print has completely dried, paint the eye with a fine brush and fabric paint. The "life" or "soul" is returned to the fish once its eye is painted. In general, the eye is painted as an outer ring of a color and an off-center inner circle of a dark color like black. A gleam of white can be added to represent reflected light.

Hand paint the eye of the fish with a small brush.

❊ TRY THIS

- *Consider using metallic paint or adding glitter or Pearl Ex to the paint to add the sheen that shows on real scales.*
- *Print more than one fish onto the same piece of fabric.*
- *Add detail and more color to the print with colored pencils, paint, or fabric markers.*
- *Print seaweed (or leaves to look like seaweed) on your fabric.*

A school of fish!

Found Object Printing

Natural Selection, by Jane Dávila

Printing with found objects can give your fabric spontaneous, unexpected, unique designs. Many household objects are suitable for use, as well as objects found in a hardware store. A bit of experimentation can yield outstanding results. When choosing found objects to print, look for interesting textures and fairly flat, even surfaces. Object surfaces that will absorb too much paint may require priming before making a final print. Don't be afraid to try a variety of objects to find the ones that appeal to you the most.

Keep an open mind and play!

Variety of found objects suitable for printing

✳ TIP

If your objects are small and hard to hold, glue them to an acrylic square or a piece of sturdy cardboard.

Supplies

- prewashed white cotton, PFD fabric, or commercial fabric
- fabric or acrylic paints
- variety of foam brushes, paint-brushes, and foam brayers
- protective covering (newsprint, plastic drop cloth, etc.)
- variety of found objects

PROCEDURE

1. Lay out your prepared fabric on a smooth, protected surface, making sure there are no wrinkles or folds in the fabric.

2. Apply one or more colors of paint to the object, smoothing out your brush strokes and avoiding excess paint.

Bubble wrap, which is available in various sizes, creates interesting textures when printed.

3. Place the painted object face down on fabric and press firmly.

Be careful not to shift or wiggle as you press to avoid blurring the print.

4. Remove the object and apply more paint to print again. If the surface becomes too clogged with paint and detail is becoming lost, wash and dry it thoroughly before applying more paint.

Metal washers in a variety of sizes

Copper tube fitting brush

Print from bubble wrap

Print from metal washers

Print from copper tube fitting brush

Lawn tractor air filter

Mushroom brush

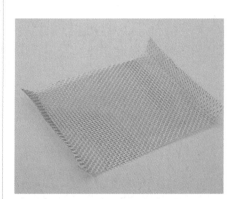

Window screening from a repair kit

Print from lawn tractor air filter

Print from mushroom brush

Print from window screening

Wire gutter strainer

Small sink basket strainer

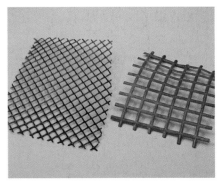

Variety of plastic meshes

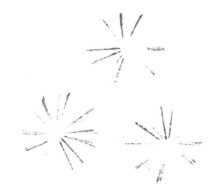

Print from wire gutter strainer

Print from sink basket strainer

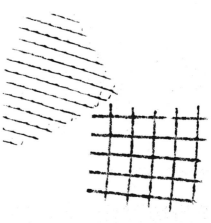

Print from plastic mesh

✹ TRY THIS

- Roll a round object to print, instead of simply pressing down.
- Take a careful look at the junk drawer (everybody has one!) in your kitchen for objects to print
- Print different objects on the same piece of fabric.
- Print the same object in different colors on the same piece of fabric
- Walk around a hardware store, garden center, or kitchen store to find interesting objects to print.

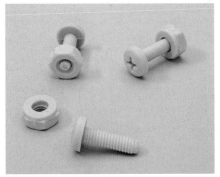

License plate bolts

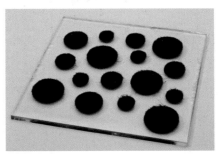

Adhesive felt pads adhered to an acrylic square base

Print from license plate bolts

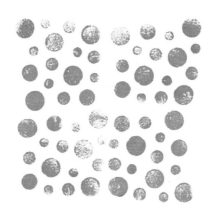

Print from adhesive felt pads

Stamp Making

Enso: either way, by Elin Waterston

It's very simple to make your own stamps. From a handful of easily obtained raw materials, you can create a stamp to use as a central motif, as a background pattern, or as an accent. Stamp your designs onto fabric with acrylic or fabric paint or with a stamp pad.

✳ TIP

Almost anything goes when choosing a fabric on which to stamp. Although fiber content is not important, you have to be careful with roughly textured fabrics and fabrics with nap. The color or print of a fabric is also not important; however, if you use a dark fabric or a heavily patterned one, make sure you use the appropriate paint. Interference colors show up very well on dark fabric, and opaque paint is perfect for both dark and patterned fabrics.

CARVED RUBBER STAMPS

Carved stamps can be highly detailed or very simple shapes. Large carved stamps, which are used for block printing, can become the subject or focal point of a work.

Variety of stamp-making materials and tools

Supplies

- Staedtler Mastercarve or Speedball Speedy Cut Carving Blocks
- linoleum cutter and blades
- pencil
- drawing paper
- stamp pad
- fabric or acrylic paint
- rubber brayer or foam brushes
- paper or fabric for testing and printing

PROCEDURE

1. Trace the outline of your block onto paper. Some blocks can be cut into pieces to make smaller stamps, if desired.

Trace the outline several times to audition multiple design options.

2. Use a pencil to draw a design within the outline.

For your first stamp, keep the design fairly simple and with thick lines. You can progress to more detailed stamps as you gain more experience.

* TIP

Your design reverses to carve and then reverses to print, so draw the design on the paper the way you'd like it to appear on fabric.

3. Turn over the drawing and place it on the block. Rub vigorously to transfer the drawing to the surface of the block. This is why the design must be drawn in pencil; pen ink won't transfer.

Use your fingers, a burnishing tool, or a spoon to transfer your drawing.

* TIP

Decide whether you will be carving the "positive" or the "negative" of your drawing—that is, are you removing the shape or the background?

The positive and the negative of the same image

4. Use a linoleum cutter to carve the areas you'd like to remove. Be especially careful around the perimeter of your drawing to create a clean line. You can choose to leave areas of background for texture.

Use the smallest blade in the linoleum cutter to start cutting, progressing to larger, wider blades as needed.

Areas of background intentionally left raised

* TIP

Consider using the back of a carving block to test how the different blades work.

5. Periodically test your progress by inking your stamp and printing on paper. You will easily be able to tell which areas need more removal and which areas are finished.

Don't clean the stamp after the test print. The inked areas will show you the areas that still need to be removed.

Test your stamp frequently. While it is always easy to remove more of the block, you won't be able to add it back if you make a mistake.

6. Clean the stamp with warm water and a nailbrush after use.

* TIP

Fabric paints usually require heat setting, but acrylics don't. Heat set the paint according to product specifications.

☀ TRY THIS

- On the thicker Mastercarve blocks, carve a positive image on one side and a negative of the same image on the other side.
- Carve two stamps meant to be used together in different colors to create one image.
- Rather than a representational image, carve a geometric design.
- Create a signature image or motif to apply to your work as a chop.

Bailemos, by Jane Dávila

Printing

1. Carved stamps can be inked with a stamp pad or with acrylic or fabric paint.

Use a stamp pad to apply ink to a stamp.

Use a rubber brayer or a foam brush to apply paint to a stamp.

2. Place the fabric face up on your work surface. Press the inked stamp face down firmly and evenly on the fabric.

Press firmly and evenly.

✳ TIP

When printing the inked stamp to fabric, it is useful to work on a slightly padded surface, like an old mouse pad or a stack of newsprint.

3. A large stamp will benefit from the use of a baren to apply even pressure.

A baren helps you get an even image.

4. A block printer's press can be used to print larger stamps. Place the fabric right side up on the lower rubber plate of the press. Place the stamp ink side down on the fabric. Press down on the handle to print.

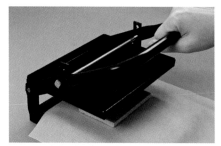

A block printer's press works on large stamps up to 6″ × 8″.

❋ **TIP**

You may need to make several proof prints before a crisp, clear image is obtained and your final print can be made.

ACRYLIC AND FOAM STAMPS

Adhesive foam cut into shapes and adhered to squares of acrylic make stamps you can see through for easy positioning. Simple to clean and reuse, these stamps are durable and versatile. Fine-detailed images are not possible, but simple shapes or patterns are ideal.

Supplies

- ■ ¹⁄₈″-thick acrylic squares: 3″ × 3″ or 4″ × 4″ for small stamps (Many glass stores and frame shops will custom cut acrylic.)
- ■ adhesive-backed craft foam sheets
- ■ scissors or an X-acto knife
- ■ pencil and drawing paper
- ■ carbon paper (optional)
- ■ stamp pad, or fabric or acrylic paint
- ■ rubber brayer or foam brushes (if using paint)
- ■ paper or fabric for testing and printing

PROCEDURE

1. Trace the outline of the acrylic square onto paper. Draw or doodle within the outline to decide on a stamp design.

Keep the design fairly simple. Because the foam is stiff, fine details are difficult.

2. Transfer the design to the back of a foam sheet. Cut the foam sheet into the necessary piece or pieces to create your design.

Transfer the design with carbon paper or redraw it on the foam sheet.

3. Peel the release paper off the back of the foam pieces and adhere them in place on your acrylic square.

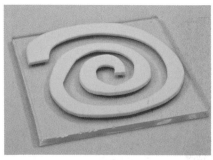

The foam is stretchy without the paper backing, so handle with care.

4. Test your stamp with a stamp pad on paper or fabric.

Ink and print several times for a sharp image.

❋ **TIP**

Allow the foam to adhere to the acrylic for a few hours before washing to ensure a strong bond.

Fabric printed with acrylic and foam stamp

☀ **TRY THIS**

- *Use these stamps for background texture to create dots, squares, lines, or chunky motifs.*
- *Create text stamps by cutting out letters to spell words. Although some companies make adhesive foam letters, these letters print backward, so you'll need to make your own.*

Printing

1. Use a stamp pad to apply ink to the stamp. Or use a foam brush or rubber brayer with acrylic or fabric paint.

Be careful to smooth out your brush strokes on the stamp for an even print.

2. Wash the stamp with warm water and a nailbrush after use. Do not allow the stamp to soak in water or the adhesive will dissolve.

FOAM "MARSHMALLOW" STAMPS

These stamps are fun and not just because they look good enough to eat! Score lines into the small round end to create a circular textured stamp. The foam is not carveable, but lines can easily be cut and portions cut away with an X-acto knife.

Supplies

- Darice Foamies 3D Shapes (large marshmallows)
- X-acto knife
- pencil and drawing paper
- stamp pad
- paper or fabric for testing and printing

Coneflower, by Jane Dávila

PROCEDURE

1. Trace the outline of your marshmallow onto paper. Doodle or draw within the outline to decide on a stamp design.

Keep the design super simple and the lines straight or gently curved.

2. Cut the lines or shape with an X-acto knife.

Cuts can be fairly shallow and will still show when printed.

3. Test your stamp with a stamp pad and paper or fabric.

For crisp images, press down firmly without shifting the stamp.

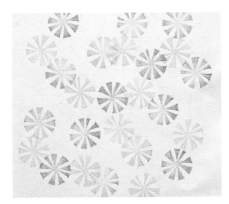

Fabric printed with a foam marshmallow stamp

☀ **TRY THIS**

■ *Print the stamp a second time before reinking for a lighter, ghost image.*
■ *Stamp multiple designs on the same fabric.*
■ *Stamp the same design in different colors.*
■ *Create the same design in different sizes as different stamps.*

Fabric Painting with Water-Based Resists

La Sirena 2, by Elin Waterston

A resist material, like wax or gutta, prohibits fabric from accepting paint. A common form of resist is wax batik. Resists permeate the fiber and, once dry, repel pigment, preventing it from adhering to the resisted areas and stopping the flow of pigment from one area to another. Areas that are painted with clear resist will remain the color of the base fabric. Resists can be applied using stamps or stencils, or they can be hand painted on with a brush or a spouted bottle. The untreated areas of the fabric are painted with diluted fabric or acrylic paint, or a wash of color is applied with a brush. Once the paint has dried and been set, the resist is removed. Water-based resists are water soluble, which means they can be washed out using warm water.

Non-water-based resists, like wax, can be used with immersion dyeing. After the resist is applied, the fabric is soaked in a dye bath. The resist is removed after the dyeing process is complete. Water-based resists will dissolve in the dye bath, so it's best not to use those for immersion dyeing.

Resists can also be used with bleach discharging. The bleach changes the color of the background fabric (dark colors usually result in the most dramatic effects), and the original color remains wherever the resist has been applied.

Representational designs and overall patterns can be painted using resists. Designs with separate areas of color require unbroken lines of resist to create enclosed shapes. This prevents the color from flowing from one area to another. Overall patterns or geometric designs can be created with or without the use of unbroken lines.

Supplies

- pencil and drawing paper
- tracing paper or vellum
- prewashed fabric
- water-based resist
- fine-tipped applicator
- fabric or acrylic paints
- small containers

- fine and broad brushes
- protective covering (newsprint, plastic drop cloth, etc.)
- stretcher bars or inexpensive embroidery hoop (optional)
- pushpins or thumbtacks for stretcher bars (optional)
- water
- paper towels

RESIST PAINTING FROM A DRAWN DESIGN

1. Draw a design on paper that you wish to recreate on fabric. Keep in mind that areas covered by the resist will remain the color of the fabric.

Draw a design on paper.

2. Trace a copy of the design on another sheet of paper or onto a piece of vellum or tracing paper. You'll use the copy when applying the resist to protect your original drawing.

> ### ■ NOTE
>
> *Do not use an ink-jet print of your design. If the ink gets wet, it can bleed onto the fabric.*

3. Place fabric over the drawing. Use the fine-tipped applicator and carefully apply the water-based resist to all areas of the design that are to remain unpainted. The resist must permeate the fibers completely to prevent the pigment from being absorbed by the fabric and to prevent the flow of paint from one enclosed shape into another.

Carefully apply resist to the fabric.

✳ TIP

If the design is difficult to see through the fabric, layer the tracing and fabric on a lightbox.

4. Allow the resist to dry thoroughly (at least 24 hours).

5. In small containers, dilute the desired colors of fabric or acrylic paint to a very watery consistency.

✳ TIP

Start with a small amount of pigment and add water gradually, testing the viscosity of the paint mixture on a scrap of prewashed fabric until it is the desired consistency. The paint should spread as soon as the brush touches the fabric. Paint looks darker when it's wet, so test your colors and allow them to dry.

6. Place the fabric on a flat, protected surface. Or attach the fabric (with pushpins or thumbtacks) to stretchers. Or put the fabric in an inexpensive hand embroidery hoop to elevate it while you paint.

7. Dip a small brush into a container of diluted paint to load the brush.

❋ TIP

Hold your brush over a paper towel while working to avoid dripping paint onto any unwanted areas.

8. Starting in a small, enclosed area, touch the brush to the fabric. The paint will spread to the resist line.

Touch the tip of your paintbrush to an enclosed area of fabric.

9. Reload the brush and add more pigment to the fabric if needed, but be careful not to overload the area or the paint will spill out over the resist line.

❋ TIP

If you're working on a flat surface, occasionally lift the fabric and move it to a clean, protected area. This helps keep the paint from lifting from the surface onto unwanted areas.

10. Allow the paint to dry completely and cure for at least 24 hours.

11. If necessary, heat set the paint according to product specifications. Fabric paints usually require heat setting, but acrylics don't.

12. Once the paint has cured and been heat set, remove the resist by washing the fabric in warm water and a mild soap.

Completed resist painting

RESIST PAINTING: FREEHAND WITH A WASH OF COLOR

1. On a protected surface, with the fabric flat, attached to stretchers, or in a hoop, create a design by applying resist freehand with the applicator.

Apply resist pattern freehand.

2. Allow the resist to dry thoroughly (at least 24 hours).

3. Dip a wide (1˝ or 2˝), flat brush into a color of diluted fabric or acrylic paints. Brush it across the fabric in broad strokes.

Paint across fabric with a wash of color.

4. Reload the brush as needed or dip a clean brush into another color and let the colors blend on the fabric.

5. Allow the paint to dry completely and cure for at least 24 hours.

6. If necessary heat set the paint according to product specifications.

7. Remove the resist by washing the fabric in warm water and a mild soap.

Completed resist-painted fabric

- Use a colored resist.
- Use Elmer's Glue Gel or potato starch as resists.

- Apply water-based resist to rubber stamps or other objects and stamp it onto fabric.
- Use oil-based media (Paintstiks or oil pastels) as a resist.

Detail of *June & the Elephant,* page 101, created using a metallic-colored resist and Dye-Na-Flow paint

Fabric painted using potato starch as a resist

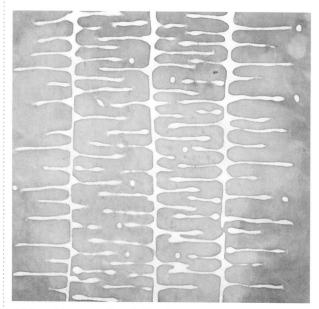

Fabric painted using Elmer's Glue Gel as a resist

Detail of *Pastiche,* page 111, created using Paintstiks as a resist

Bleach Discharging

cielo, **by Elin Waterston**

Discharging is a form of surface design in which color is removed (instead of added) to create patterns or designs. Household bleach, which is available in various forms, is an effective product for color removal. Bleach causes a chemical reaction in fabric that alters the color. Different fabrics will react to bleach differently, both in the time needed for the reaction to take place and in the resulting color. Some fabric will take more time to react, while other fabrics will take less time. Watch the fabric and try to gauge how much color has discharged. Don't leave the bleach on for more than about 10 minutes or you might damage the fabric. Different tones, brands, and shades of the same color might each discharge to different colors and to different degrees. You never really know what color you're going to get! It's not unusual for a

black cotton to discharge to blue, orange, white, purple, or red. Dark or deeply saturated solid colors will yield the most dramatic results, but discharging can be done on medium and light colors and printed fabric as well.

Fabrics of the same color will not always discharge to the same color.

Whether fabric is prewashed or unwashed will also affect the discharge process. If there is sizing in unwashed fabric, bleach might bead up on the surface. If the fabric has been prewashed to remove the sizing, bleach might seep into the fibers and spread. It's important to experiment and expect mistakes. Bleach discharging is unpredictable—that's all part of the look of this technique. As with any surface design method, experimentation is key.

Once the color has been discharged, the bleach has to be rinsed out and neutralized or else it will keep bleaching forever. Several commercial brands of neutralizers, which halt the bleaching action, are available, including Bleach-Stop and Anti-Chlor. A solution of one part white vinegar to three parts water will also neutralize the bleach. Once the bleach action is stopped, fabric needs to be washed in clear water or water with a mild detergent.

Supplies

- 8″ × 8″ to 10″ × 10″ squares of fabric in various colors—solids and prints, prewashed and unwashed

- bleach pen or bleach gel cleanser, such as Soft Scrub

- diluted bleach (about one part bleach to two parts water, but try different recipes to see which work best for you)

- clean spray bottle

- small containers

- lace, netting, cheesecloth, washers, leaves, coins, or other items to mask areas of fabric

- large, inexpensive paintbrush

- rubber gloves (and other protective gear, if needed)

- protective covering (newsprint, plastic drop cloth sheets, etc.)

- basin with clean water

- basin with bleach-neutralizing solution (Anti-Chlor, Bleach-Stop, one part vinegar to three parts water)

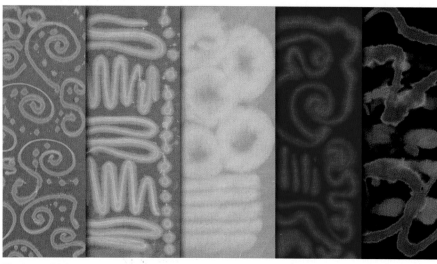

Discharged fabrics

◼ NOTE

When discharging large pieces of fabric, it's a good idea to work quickly and in small sections. The bleach action is quick. If you're working on too large an area, the first area of bleached fabric will need to be neutralized before the you finish bleaching the rest of the yardage.

◼ SAFETY NOTE

Always use caution when using chemicals. Even household bleach can be dangerous or toxic if used incorrectly or without safety precautions. Work outside, wear protective gear (i.e., gloves, goggles, and a respirator, if necessary), and keep all chemicals away from children and animals.

BLEACH PEN AND GEL CLEANSER DISCHARGING

1. Lay fabric flat on a protected surface.

2. Draw designs with the bleach pen or squeeze out designs with gel cleanser.

3. Watch the fabric to gauge how much color has discharged. Do not leave the bleach on for more than about 10 minutes. Remember that colors appear darker when wet.

4. When you are ready to stop the bleaching action, rinse the fabric in clear water.

5. Soak the fabric in a neutralizing solution for 5–15 minutes, stirring occasionally.

6. Wash the fabric in clear water or water with a mild detergent.

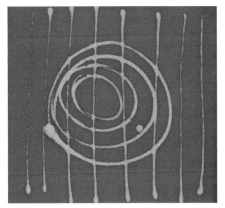

Discharged fabric made by drawing with a bleach pen

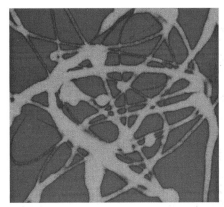

Discharged fabric made by squeezing bleach gel onto fabric

SPRAYED BLEACH DISCHARGING

1. Lay fabric flat on a protected surface.

2. Place an open-textured item, such as netting or lace, or solid items, such as leaves, washers, or coins, on the fabric.

3. Spray the fabric with a diluted bleach solution from a spray bottle.

4. Watch and gauge the amount of color discharge. Do not leave the bleach on for more than about 10 minutes.

5. When you are ready to stop the bleaching action, remove the mask items and rinse the fabric in clear water.

6. Soak the fabric in a neutralizing solution for 5–15 minutes, stirring occasionally.

7. Wash the fabric in clear water or water with a mild detergent.

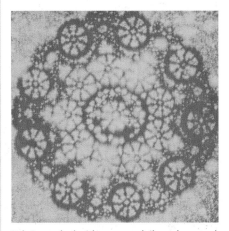

Fabric masked with a paper doily and sprayed with bleach solution

Fabric masked with small wood squares and sprayed with bleach solution

BRUSHED BLEACH DISCHARGING

1. Lay the fabric flat (or scrunch it into a ball) on a protected surface.

2. Dip a wide paintbrush into a container filled with diluted bleach and brush it across the fabric.

Apply diluted bleach with a wide paintbrush.

3. Watch and gauge the amount of color discharge. Do not leave the bleach on for more than about 10 minutes.

4. When you are ready to stop the bleaching action, rinse the fabric in clear water.

5. Soak the fabric in a neutralizing solution for 5–15 minutes, stirring occasionally.

6. Wash the fabric in clear water or water with a mild detergent.

✳ TIP

When pressing bleached fabric, use low heat. Bleach-discharged fibers are delicate and could break down if too much heat is applied.

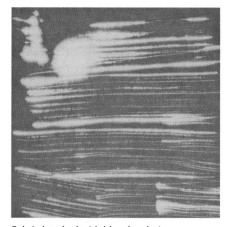

Fabric brushed with bleach solution

◉ NOTE

Bleach is strong and can be very destructive on certain fibers. Always do a test on a small swatch of fabric. Do not use bleach on silk or wool.

❂ TRY THIS

- *Add a thickening agent to the bleach and block print or stamp bleach on fabric.*
- *Hang fabric outside on a clothes line or inside over a bathtub. Squirt bleach gel across the top edge. Let the bleach drip down, making discharged streaks.*

Fabric stamped with bleach gel

- *Mask areas of fabric and apply bleach gel to the unmasked areas, spreading it with a disposable brush or your fingers. Wear gloves!*

Fabric squirted with bleach gel

- *Create a mottled look by dipping scrunched up fabric in a basin of diluted bleach (about one part bleach to four parts water).*
- *Brush or stamp bleach onto commercially printed fabric.*

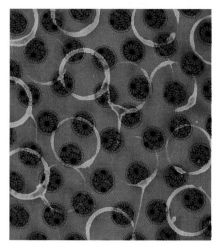

Bleach gel applied to a commercially printed fabric

Images on Fabric

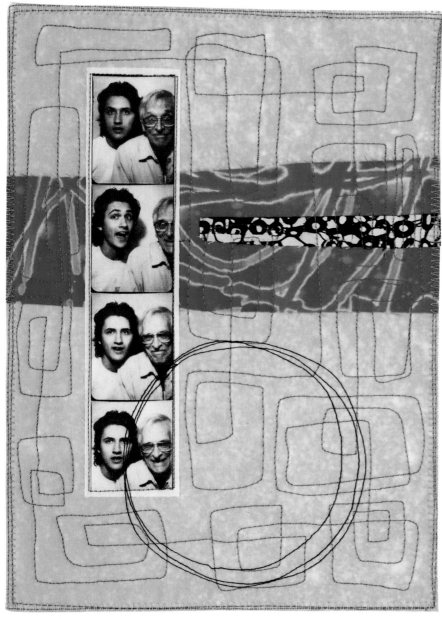

At the Warhol, **by Elin Waterston**

Treating fabric yourself with Bubble Jet Set takes a little more advanced preparation but is more cost effective than the pretreated fabric. Soak the fabric in the Bubble Jet Set solution according to the manufacturer's instructions and stabilize (with freezer paper or a full-sheet adhesive label). Print on it using an ink-jet printer.

Some ink-jet printers use pigment-based inks that don't require any pretreatment of the fabric. This allows you to print on your choice of fabric, whether commercially printed or dyed, without any special preparation. Stabilize fabric with freezer paper or an adhesive label.

Another option is to print photographs and images onto transfer paper to transfer them to fabric. You can choose from several brands of transfer papers, including Paper Magic Group PhotoFusion Paper. Each brand will have specific instructions. However, with most transfer papers, you simply print a mirror image of your photo onto the paper and press it onto the front side of your fabric.

These are just a few of the many ways of transferring photos and images onto fabric. Whatever your method of choice, you'll need to experiment with your computer and printer settings to see what will give you the best results. Follow the directions specific to the product you're using.

PRINTING AND TRANSFERRING PHOTOS

Photographs or digital images can be printed directly onto fabric using an ink-jet printer. Numerous brands of ready-to-use pretreated fabric are available. Each brand has a variety of fabric types for printing, including cotton, silk, and organza, most of which are white or natural. The fabric comes mounted on a paper backing, which stabilizes the fabric for printing.

▥ *Print text on fabric and incorporate it into your designs.*

▥ *Create digital collages to print on fabric.*

▥ *Print a direct scan of an object.*

Detail of *Enso: high in the haze,* page 109, digital collage printed on fabric

Journal page with an image of a camera which was scanned and printed on fabric

IMAGE TRANSFER WITH TRANSPARENCY SHEETS

Photos, images, and text printed onto transparency film can be transferred to fabric (or paper) using gel medium or water. This method of image transfer is unpredictable, but don't worry about mistakes and imperfections—they give each piece individuality and character!

GEL MEDIUM TRANSFER

> **◉ NOTE**
>
> *Gel medium gives the fabric a sheen and makes it slightly rubbery.*

Supplies

- ink-jet printable transparency sheets
- matte gel medium
- foam brush
- foam roller
- prewashed fabric
- freezer paper
- baren or burnishing tool

1. Iron freezer paper to the back of the fabric to stabilize it.

2. Print your desired images onto a transparency sheet (with the image reversed), following the manufacturer's directions.

Original black bird drawing

I guess my little bird can sing #1, by Elin Waterston

Multiple images of the black bird drawing printed on a transparency sheet

3. Cut out the image, leaving some space around the edges.

4. Apply a thin, even coat of gel medium to the fabric with a foam brush.

5. Smooth out the gel medium with a foam roller.

6. Place a transparency sheet ink side down on the treated area of fabric. Use a baren or burnishing tool to transfer the image. It can be helpful to hold the transparency sheet in place while burnishing.

Transfer the image by burnishing the transparency sheet.

7. Slowly peel off the transparency sheet.

8. Allow the gel medium to dry.

Image transferred using transparency film and gel medium

✳ TIP

If you use too much medium, the image will smear. If you don't use enough, the image will not transfer. You'll learn from experience how much medium to apply.

✳ TIP

Always use a pressing cloth when ironing a transferred image.

WATER TRANSFER

Supplies

- ink-jet printable transparency sheets

- prewashed fabric

- freezer paper

- spray bottle

- baren or burnishing tool

1. Iron freezer paper to the back of the fabric to stabilize it.

2. Print the desired images onto the transparency sheet (with the image reversed), following the manufacturer's directions.

3. Cut out the image, leaving some space around the edges.

4. Holding the image vertically, evenly spray the printed side with water.

Make sure to cover the entire surface of the image with water.

5. Quickly place the wet image ink side down on the fabric. Use a baren or burnishing tool to transfer the image. Don't allow the transparency sheet to shift while burnishing or the image will be blurry!

Transfer the image by burnishing the transparency sheet.

6. Lift up one corner of the transparency sheet to check the progress of the transfer. When the transfer is complete, peel away the transparency sheet and allow the fabric to dry. This type of transfer results in a pale image.

Image transferred using transparency sheet and water

⊙ **NOTE**

If any part of the image fails to transfer, hold one corner of the transparency in place. Then add a little bit of water and burnish again.

☀ **TRY THIS**

- *Spray the fabric with water instead of spraying the transparency sheet to transfer the image.*
- *Print text or images on transparency film and apply it directly to your artwork.*

Circus-themed trading card, by Elin Waterston, using an image printed on transparency film

CHAPTER **TWO:**
SPECIAL EFFECTS

"While I recognize the necessity for a basis of observed reality—true art lies in a reality that is felt." – **Odilon Redon**

experiment—(v.) to try something new, especially in order to gain experience (from Latin *experimentum*: a trial; from *experiri*: to test, try)

Comet 2, by Elin Waterston

Paintstiks

Shiva Artist's Paintstiks are pigments mixed with refined linseed oil solidified in wax. These solid oil colors can be applied directly to fabric or spread with your finger, a brush, or a palette knife. Colors can be mixed and blended on a palette or directly on the painted surface. Paintstiks are self sealing—a film forms on the stick when exposed to air to prevent the paint from drying out. Before using a Paintstik, remove this film by pinching and twisting the end of the Paintstik with a paper towel or carefully carving it away with a knife or your fingernail.

Paintstiks are great for a variety of surfaces, including canvas, paper, wood, plastic, and metal—as well as fabric. The paint dries flexible, only slightly altering the hand of the fabric or not at all, depending on the thickness of the pigment application. Paintstiks can be cleaned up with either soap and water or turpentine.

Shiva Paintstiks

Supplies

- Shiva Artist's Paintstiks, regular or iridescent
- prewashed fabrics in various solid colors
- paper towels
- rubbing plates, lace, or other textured items
- masking tape
- nonslip pad, freezer paper, or full-sheet adhesive label to stabilize fabric
- stencils or masks made from freezer paper, iron-on stabilizer, or adhesive labels
- natural wood or rough-surfaced palette (glass and plastic are too smooth)
- blender or stencil brushes
- drawing pencil
- small paintbrush (optional, for fine details)
- unprinted newsprint or paper bags
- protective covering (newsprint, plastic drop cloth, etc.)
- iron

TEXTURE RUBBING

Rubbing the Paintstiks across a textured surface re-creates the texture on the surface of the fabric. Find interesting textured items, like wood grain and lace, or use commercially available rubbing plates.

Items with interesting textures, as well as rubbing plates, can be used for rubbings.

1. Place prewashed fabric on a textured surface or rubbing plate. Tape it in place if needed.

Lay fabric over textured surface.

Tape fabric in place.

2. Remove the cardboard tube from the Paintstik and peel away the protective film.

3. Applying even pressure, drag the side of a Paintstik across the fabric, in 1 smooth pass. Take care not to let the fabric or rubbing plate slip out of place.

Drag the Paintstik across the fabric.

4. Move on to an unpainted area of fabric and repeat Step 3.

5. Add layers of additional textures and colors as desired.

6. Allow the pigment to dry fully (3–5 days).

7. Heat set by placing newsprint or a paper bag over the painted area. Turn over the fabric and press from the back side with a hot, dry iron for 10–15 seconds to heat set.

STENCILS AND MASKS

Paintstiks can be used with stencils and masks. You can create your own stencils and masks using freezer paper, iron-on stabilizer, or adhesive labels that can be attached to the surface of the fabric.

1. Secure the stencil or mask onto the front of the fabric.

2. Stabilize prewashed fabric by placing it on a nonslip pad or by pressing freezer paper or attaching a full-sheet adhesive label to the back side.

3. Apply pigment to the unmasked area. Rub the pigment onto a rough-surfaced palette and use a stencil brush to brush the pigment away from the edges of the stencil. Or rub the end of the Paintstik directly on the fabric.

Apply pigment to the unmasked areas directly or with a stencil or blender brush.

4. Carefully lift the stencil off the fabric.

5. Allow the pigment to dry fully (3–5 days).

6. Place newsprint or a paper bag over the painted area. Turn over the fabric and press from the back side with a hot, dry iron for 10–15 seconds to heat set.

Design created by applying Paintstiks directly, using a freezer paper stencil

Design created by applying Paintstiks with a stencil brush, using a freezer paper stencil

✳ **TIP**

Varying the pressure and amount of pigment will create shading and dimensionality.

DIRECT APPLICATION: FREEHAND PAINTING

An image, motif, or design (representational or abstract) can be applied directly by using Paintstiks just as you would use pastels or crayons—coloring in areas, shading, and adding detail. Because of the thickness of the Paintstiks, it is difficult to get fine details. If fine detail work is required, apply the pigment using a small paintbrush.

Original rooster sketch

1. Stabilize prewashed fabric by placing it on a nonslip pad or by pressing freezer paper or attaching a full-sheet adhesive label to the back side.

2. Lightly draw the desired design on the fabric in pencil.

3. Paint in the design with Paintstiks, blending and adding layers as needed.

Paint in the design by applying Paintstiks directly or with a brush.

4. Allow the pigment to dry fully (3–5 days).

5. Place newsprint or a paper bag over the painted area. Turn over the fabric and press from the back side with a hot, dry iron for 10–15 seconds to heat set.

Completed rooster painting

◎ **NOTE**

Fabric that is painted with Paintstiks should not be dry-cleaned.

☀ **TRY THIS**

- *Use Paintstiks to create abstract patterns and visual textures.*

Detail of *12.12,* page 79, made by applying Paintstiks in random, abstract patterns

- *Apply pigment after quilting.*

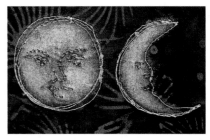

Detail of *Zoom,* page 95, made with Paintstiks applied after quilting

Fabric Inks

Kismet, by Jane Dávila

Fabric inks are wonderful for detail work or for broad strokes of color. Some inks can also be used to marble fabric and to create a dyed effect. Other inks can antique or distress the look of fabric. Still others can add glimmering highlights and metallic or pearlescent effects. All fabric inks have a minimal effect on the hand or softness of the fabric, and many are permanent after heat setting.

TSUKINEKO ALL-PURPOSE INKS

An assortment of Tsukineko inks

Supplies

- Tsukineko All-Purpose Inks

- prewashed, light-colored, white cotton fabric or PFD fabric

- paintbrushes and foam brushes

- fabric markers, such as Fabrico Dual-Tip fabric markers

- foam shaving cream

- large shallow pan

- wooden skewer

- scraper or piece of template plastic about 3″ × 5″

- freezer paper

- spray bottle

- protective covering (newsprint, plastic drop cloth, etc.)

- iron

DIRECT PAINTING

1. Use a small or large paintbrush to apply ink to fabric.

Iron a piece of freezer paper to the back of the fabric to stabilize it.

> ◉ **NOTE**
>
> *Heat set between colors, if desired, to prevent bleeding or blending of colors.*

2. Heat setting with a hot, dry iron will make the ink permanent and washable.

DIRECT PAINTING WITH MARKER RESIST

1. Use fabric markers as a resist to outline a shape or form. Heat set the marker lines before applying ink.

Use a matching or contrasting marker, depending on the desired effect.

2. Use a paintbrush to apply ink to the fabric.

3. Heat setting with a hot, dry iron will make the ink permanent and washable.

MARBLING

1. Cover the bottom of a shallow pan with a layer of foam shaving cream. Smooth it out with a scraper.

The layer of shaving cream should be about 1″ thick.

2. Use a paintbrush or a wooden skewer to drop ink into the shaving cream.

Use two or more colors of ink.

3. Drag a wooden skewer upright through the shaving cream, creating patterns and swirls.

Don't overdo the dragging, otherwise the pattern will become indistinct and the colors muddy.

Fabric background will show through in areas without ink.

4. Place the prewashed fabric face down on the surface of the shaving cream.

Don't lift or move the fabric once it has touched the surface of the shaving cream.

5. Press lightly but evenly with your hands so that all of the fabric comes in contact with the shaving cream.

If the surface of the shaving cream is not perfectly smooth, don't worry! Use your hands to press the fabric flat to the surface. The shaving cream will "give" and flatten out.

You will know that you have made good contact with the ink when you see it start to come through the back of the fabric.

6. Lift the fabric out of the shaving cream and place it on a clean, protected surface.

Don't panic! The fabric may look like a mess, but everything is fine. The design will be revealed in the next step.

7. Scrape the excess shaving cream from the fabric to see the marbling pattern formed by the swirled ink. Deposit the excess shaving cream into your shallow pan to discard or rub it onto another piece of fabric for a muted wash of color.

Scrape every bit of shaving cream off the fabric and allow the fabric to air dry.

This method yields fabric that's a little less intense than the original ink colors due to their dilution with the shaving cream.

8. It isn't necessary or advisable to rinse the fabric. Simply let it air dry completely and then heat set with a dry iron.

☀ TRY THIS

- *Create different patterns by dragging the skewer in only horizontal, vertical, or diagonal directions.*
- *Leave large, open background areas by doing minimal dragging of the skewer. Or drag the ink into every corner of the shaving cream to cover more of the background fabric.*
- *Use complementary colors of ink for dramatic results.*

"DYED" WASHES

1. Dampen prewashed fabric by spraying it with water.

2. With a foam brush or paintbrush, apply ink to the surface of the wet fabric, using a loose hand and broad strokes. This "dyed" fabric makes a wonderful background, and the ink leaves the fabric soft instead of stiff like painted fabrics.

Use more than one color of ink.

Add more water for a paler effect.

3. After the fabric is completely dry, heat set with an iron.

ANTIQUING, DISTRESSING, AND GLIMMER MIST INKS

Antiquing and distressing inks add a sense of age and wear to fabric. They can tone down a too-bright color or blend disparate colors together. Glimmer Mist Inks add a dash of glitz and a subtle wash of color. Do not use any of these inks if you desire a tightly controlled result. These inks are perfect for somewhat organic, uneven, and unpredictable effects. Heat setting with a hot, dry iron will help these inks be more water-resistant, but the results are not washable nor are they permanent.

Assortment of antiquing, distressing, and Glimmer inks

Supplies

- Tattered Angels Glimmer Mist or Tsukineko Walnut Spray Ink

- Ranger Distress Ink stamp pads

- prewashed fabric

- protective covering (newsprint, plastic drop cloth, etc.)

- freezer paper for cutting masks

- iron

SPRAY PATTERNS

Shake Glimmer Mist or Walnut Ink, then spray evenly or randomly over the surface of your prewashed fabric or a finished project.

Fabric before spraying Walnut Ink

Fabric after spraying Willow Walnut Ink

SPRAY PATTERNS USING A MASK

1. Mask an area of fabric with freezer paper. Iron to set the mask in place.

2. Spray open areas of the fabric with Glimmer Mist or Walnut Ink.

Area masked off with freezer paper

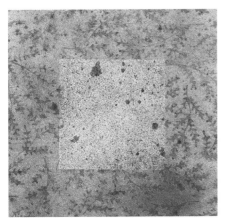

Midnight Blue Glimmer Mist applied to fabric over and around masked area

Mask removed

 TIP

Place plastic, fabric, or paper to protect the surrounding areas of your working space from overspray. If you use paper or fabric, it will develop interesting colors and textures from the overspray and can be used in another project.

 **TRY THIS**

- Tear freezer paper to create a mask with a very organic edge
- Spray a piece of fabric before cutting it for use in a quilt.

DISTRESSED SURFACES AND EDGES

1. Rub Distress Ink stamp pad onto the surface of a fabric. The color of the fabric will become muted and will look aged.

Fabric before applying Distress Ink

Fabric after applying Tea Dye Distress Ink

2. Rub the Distress Ink stamp pad along the edges of a finished element or piece for a distressed, worn-out look. The results are not washable.

Fabric before applying Distress Ink

Fabric after applying Fired Brick Distress Ink

METALLIC SHELLAC INKS AND PEARLESCENT LIQUID ACRYLIC INKS

Even if sparkle and shine aren't your thing, using a little glimmer or a hint of metallic ink can add depth to your work. Metallic ink can be used to create allover patterns or to add small details to specific areas. They are particularly effective on dark fabrics.

Allover pattern created with pearlescent ink

Allover pattern created with metallic ink

Assortment of metallic and pearlescent inks

Supplies

- metallic Sennelier Shellac Ink or Daler-Rowney Pearlescent Liquid Acrylic Ink
- prewashed fabric
- fine paintbrushes
- protective covering (newsprint, plastic drop cloth, etc.)

PROCEDURE

Use a fine paintbrush to apply metallic or pearlescent ink to fabric. Be certain to shake the bottles well before and during use, as the heavier metallic particles will settle to the bottom of the bottles. The treated fabric should never be heat set; the results are not washable.

 TRY THIS

Use metallic or pearlescent inks in addition to fabric inks when marbling with shaving cream (see page 54).

Water-Soluble Pastels

11am, by Elin Waterston

Several brands and types of water-soluble pastels are currently available. These pastels are useful for adding color, detail, and shading to existing elements; drawing images; creating patterns and designs; or creating an overall wash of color. Water-soluble pastels are soft, blendable, and easy to work with. They are most suited for use in small areas. Caran d'Ache Neocolor II Artists' Crayons are water-soluble wax pastels. Neocolors are not washable; heat setting will not render them permanent. Cretacolor AquaStics are water-soluble oil pastels that can be heat set for permanence, although washing is not recommended. A measure of water resistance can be gained by mixing in a small amount of gel medium with the water used for blending either type of pastel. Both Neocolors and AquaStics are available in sets or individually in a wide variety of colors, including metallics.

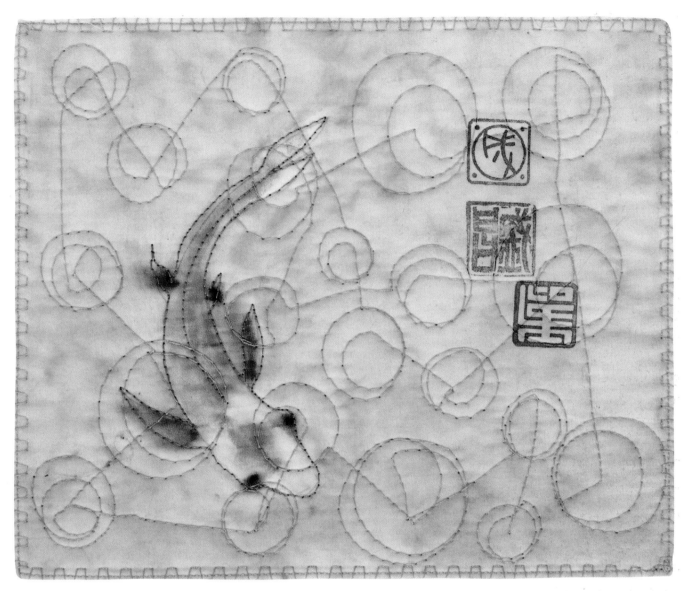

Mizu 2, by Elin Waterston

Either brand of pastels can be applied in a number of ways. For example, you can apply color with a dry pastel and lightly spray with water or release color with a wet brush for a wash of color.

Color can also be applied by dipping pastels in water and drawing on dry fabric (which will result in saturated color and a hard line) or on wet fabric.

Design drawn using water-soluble pastels

Pastel applied dry and sprayed with water

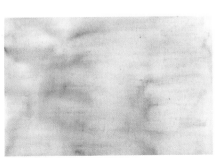

Pastel applied dry and blended with a wet brush

Painted Fusible Web

Somnolence, by Elin Waterston

Pellon Wonder-Under fusible web can be painted with fabric or acrylic paint and fused to fabric, adding layers of color and creating interesting texture or design elements on the fabric surface. Paint diluted with water will create a transparent effect, whereas full-strength paint will have a more opaque look. The results of this technique are somewhat unpredictable and will create an organic, imperfect effect.

Supplies

- Pellon Wonder-Under fusible web (regular weight)
- fabric or acrylic paint
- paintbrush
- container of water
- prewashed fabric
- protective covering (newsprint, plastic drop cloth, etc.)
- scissors
- iron
- appliqué pressing sheet or parchment paper

1. Work on a protected surface as you apply fabric or acrylic paint, in desired strength, to the web side of a piece of Wonder-Under. Cover the entire piece with paint.

Apply paint

2. Allow the paint to dry.

3. Cut out or tear desired shapes from the painted fusible web.

4. Place the painted fusible with the web side down on the background fabric or on a pieced/collaged quilt top. Cover the painted shape with a pressing sheet or parchment paper to protect your iron. Fuse with a dry iron for 15–30 seconds.

5. Allow the fabric to cool completely.

6. Slowly and carefully peel away the paper.

✳ TIP

The web must be completely cool for the paper to peel away properly.

7. Add other collage elements to complete your design.

✳ TIP

After the painted fusible web is adhered to the fabric, do not wash the fabric or press it unless you use a pressing sheet or parchment paper to protect your iron.

☀ TRY THIS

- *Use Jacquard Lumiere paint for a metallic look.*
- *Blend multiple colors of paint.*
- *Add Jacquard Pearl Ex Powdered Pigments to the wet paint for a pearlescent sheen.*
- *Experiment with different types of paint, colors of background fabrics, and cutting versus tearing painted shapes.*

Gel Medium

Golden Soft Gel Medium is an extremely versatile tool for the art quilter. It can be used as an extender for acrylic paints, as an adhesive for fabric and paper, as a sealing top coat, and to change a finish. It can also be used to transfer ink-jet images to fabric (see page 47). Gel medium is an excellent adhesive as it does not discolor or become brittle with time. When used as a sealant, it provides a measure of protection against harmful ultraviolet rays.

Golden Soft Gel Medium and foam brushes

Supplies

- Golden Soft Gel Medium (matte, semigloss, or gloss finish)
- paintbrush or foam brush
- prewashed fabric
- protective covering (newsprint, plastic drop cloth, etc.)

GEL MEDIUM AS AN ADHESIVE

Apply a thin, even coat of gel medium to the back of a piece of paper or fabric. Press firmly to a background. Once dry, the medium can easily be sewn through, although it isn't necessary.

Apply gel medium to the back of a piece of paper or fabric.

Press firmly in place and weight down, if necessary, while drying.

✳ TIP

Always clean brushes thoroughly with warm water and soap. Do not allow the gel medium to dry on the brush.

GEL MEDIUM AS A TOPCOAT OR SEALANT

Use a paintbrush or foam brush to apply a thin, even coat of gel medium to any surface you wish to protect. Once dry, the gel medium will render the surface water- and UV-resistant. Used as a topcoat, the gel medium can also change the sheen of a surface or object.

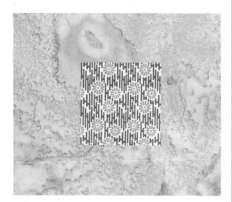

Fabric before applying gel medium

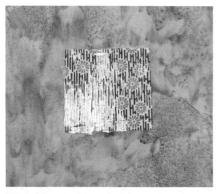

Fabric after applying semigloss gel medium

❋ TRY THIS

- *Add a small amount of acrylic or fabric paint to the gel medium to create a translucent glaze.*
- *Mix with acrylic paint and use it to create surface texture on a fabric. It will hold soft peaks when dry.*
- *Use gel medium to transfer ink-jet images (see page 47) from cardstock or transparencies to fabric.*

Expandable Paint Medium

Sunny Days, **by Jane Dávila**

Create spectacular patterns in relief on fabric and add textured dimension with paint. There are two basic methods of application. The first is to apply the expandable paint medium and then to overpaint with acrylic paint after it is dry. This method will result in stronger, brighter colors, although you'll need to be careful to cover the entire medium with paint, as the medium will dry to a beige color. In the second method, mix the medium with the paint before applying it to your fabric. This method will result in paler, more pastel colors.

In both methods, the finishing step is the same: heat is applied to the dry paint, and the medium expands. Use machine stitching to define the edges and contours of the painted design to call attention to the relief.

Supplies

- Pebeo Setacolor expandable paint medium
- Pebeo Setacolor transparent paint or other acrylic paint
- prewashed fabric
- paintbrush
- iron, heat gun, or hair dryer
- protective covering (newsprint, plastic drop cloth, etc.)

Method 1 results

Method 2 results with the same paint color

METHOD 1

1. Use a brush to apply expandable paint medium to a fabric that is placed on a protected surface. Allow the fabric to dry for approximately 30 minutes.

Applying the paint medium unevenly, with ridges and thick spots, will result in interesting texture once the medium is expanded.

2. Apply paint over the dried paint medium. Allow the paint to dry before proceeding.

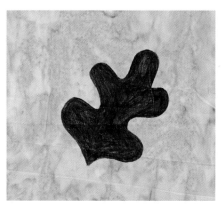

Be careful to cover all of the expandable paint medium or you'll have unsightly beige spots on the finished piece.

3. Expand the medium by ironing on the reverse side or by using a hair dryer or heat gun. The painted medium is water resistant after you fix it with an iron.

Finished fabric after expanding

METHOD 2

1. Mix expandable paint medium with transparent paint and apply it to your fabric. Allow the fabric to dry for approximately 30 minutes.

2. Expand the medium by ironing on the reverse side or by using a hair dryer or heat gun. The medium is water resistant after being fixed with an iron.

Finished fabric after expanding

✳ **TRY THIS**

- *Use expandable paint medium to create realistic tree bark or rocks.*
- *A faux trapunto effect can be achieved with expandable paint medium.*

Shrink Film

Sea life Artist Trading Card with a shrink film turtle, by Elin Waterston

Shrink film is a specialty film product that can be used to create one-of-a-kind embellishments. Images or text can be drawn, painted, stamped, or printed onto shrink film using acrylic paints, inks, colored pencils, and permanent markers. Once a design has been applied, the film is cut out and baked in a conventional oven or a toaster oven. When baked, the film shrinks to a thick, hard plastic, about one-third to one-half its original size.

Shrink film is available in clear, white, or black; matte or gloss finish; and ink-jet printable.

Embellishments made with shrink film

Supplies

- Grafix Shrink Film
- Grafix Ink Jet Shrink Film
- drawing pencil and paper
- colored pencils, acrylic paint, inks, and permanent markers
- fine sandpaper
- paper scissors or an X-acto knife
- 1/4″ hole punch
- parchment paper
- ink-jet printer

SHRINK FILM: HAND DRAWN

1. Draw a design 2–3 times larger than the desired finished size on a piece of paper.

Draw your design on paper.

2. Lightly sand the surface of the shrink film with fine sandpaper to rough the surface.

3. Trace the design onto the shrink film with a permanent marker or colored pencil.

4. Color in your design using your media of choice. The color will intensify as the film shrinks.

5. Cut out the design with scissors (not your best scissors) or an X-acto knife.

6. Use a ¼″ hole punch to punch one or more holes for later attachment (if desired) at least ¼″ from the cut edge.

7. Preheat a toaster (or conventional) oven to 250°–400°.

8. Place decorated shrink film in the oven on a cooking tray lined with parchment paper. Bake for 2–3 minutes.

 ✳ TIP

Covering film with a piece of parchment paper during the baking process will lessen the likelihood of the film curling and sticking to itself. However, it makes it more difficult to monitor the shrinking process.

NOTE

Monitor this process closely so as not to overcook the piece. The film will curl up and then flatten out again while it's cooking. It's wicked cool.

9. Remove the film from the oven when the piece is flat. Caution: It will be hot!

10. Allow to cool.

✳ TIP

If the piece is not quite flat when you remove it from the oven, press it flat with a spatula or the bottom of a drinking glass while still hot.

NOTE

Shrink film doesn't shrink perfectly every time. Expect some distortion.

SHRINK FILM: INK-JET PRINTED

1. Create a design or select a photograph to print. Remember that the color intensifies as the film shrinks.

2. Print the design onto ink-jet printable shrink film.

3. Cut out the design with scissors or an X-acto knife.

Original designs, created in Adobe Photoshop, printed onto shrink film

4. Use a ¼″ hole punch to punch one or more holes for later attachment (if desired) at least ¼″ from the cut edge.

5. Preheat a toaster (or conventional) oven to 250°–400°.

6. Place the decorated shrink film in the oven on a cooking tray lined with parchment paper. Bake for 2–3 minutes.

7. Remove the film from the oven when the piece is flat. Caution: It will be hot!

8. Allow the piece to cool.

Printed film before and after shrinking process: note the difference in size and color from the original.

☀ **TRY THIS**

- Rubber stamp or block print designs on shrink film.
- Use a heat gun to shrink film.
- Remove film from the heat before the shrinking process is complete (i.e., when it's still curly).

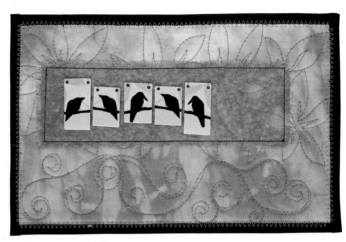

Gathering, by Elin Waterston

Metallic Foil and Leafing

Metallic foil is a thin layer of colored, metallic plastic attached to a layer of cellophane that can be applied with glue or fusible web or with bonding powder. Metal leafing is an extremely thin layer of genuine or imitation gold, silver, or copper. Gel medium can be used to apply metal leafing to fabric with a stamp, stencil, or free-form painting. Because the foils and leafings are so thin, the texture of the fabric they're applied to will affect the finished result. A smooth fabric will have a smooth metallic finish, whereas a more textured fabric will have a more textured finish. Some types of metallic foils may be washable, though this isn't recommended. Metal leafing is never washable, as it's entirely too fragile.

METALLIC FOILS

Metallic foils and glues

All Who Wander, by Jane Dávila

Supplies

- Jones Tones Foil Paper
- fusible web, foil glue, or Bo-Nash 007 Bonding Powder
- prewashed fabric
- paper scissors
- pressing cloth, appliqué pressing sheet, or parchment paper
- paintbrush or sponge applicator (optional)
- burnishing tool (optional)
- iron

Foiling with Fusible Web

1. Cut out or tear desired shapes from fusible web.

Shape cut from fusible web

2. Fuse the web to the right side of the fabric following the manufacturer's directions.

3. Peel off the fusible's paper backing and place a sheet of foil color side up so it covers the entire fusible web shape. (If you're using silver, place it shiny side up.)

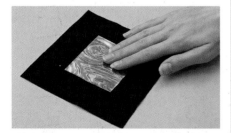

Place the foil on the exposed fusible web shape.

4. Cover the foil sheet with a pressing cloth and press for about 10 seconds with a medium hot iron.

5. Let the fabric cool completely before peeling off the foil sheet.

The foil is removed from the cellophane in the shape of the fusible web.

Foiling with Glue

1. Apply foil glue to the fabric with a brush or a sponge or directly from the applicator bottle.

Apply glue smoothly and evenly.

2. Allow the glue to dry completely—until it's clear.

3. Place a sheet of foil color side up (or, if you're using silver, shiny side up) so it covers the area of glue.

4. Rub with your fingers or a burnishing tool.

Burnish the foil sheet.

5. Peel off the foil sheet.

The foil is removed from the cellophane where the glue was applied.

Foiling with Bonding Powder

1. Sprinkle bonding powder onto your fabric.

Use a lot of bonding powder or a little, depending on the effect desired.

✳ TIP

This technique produces beautiful starry night skies and random sparkles. Experiment with different colors of foil.

2. Place a sheet of foil color side up (or, if you're using silver, shiny side up) so it covers all of the bonding powder.

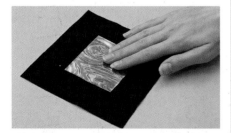

Foil on bonding powder

3. Cover the foil sheet with a pressing cloth and press for about 10 seconds with a medium hot iron.

4. Let the fabric cool completely before peeling off the foil sheet.

Peel foil to reveal sparkles.

☀ **TRY THIS**

Apply glue to a stamp and stamp it onto fabric. Allow the glue to dry. Then place a sheet of foil over it and burnish.

Stamped images with foil

METAL LEAFING

Variety of gold, silver, and copper metal leafing

Supplies

- genuine or imitation metal leafing
- gel medium
- paintbrush
- freezer paper to use as a mask or stencil (optional)
- prewashed fabric
- soft cloth or soft brush

PROCEDURE

1. Apply gel medium to the fabric—freehand, with a paintbrush, or using a freezer paper mask.

Apply gel medium in a thin, smooth coat, avoiding brush strokes.

2. Gently tap the metal leafing onto the fresh surface of the gel medium.

The leafing is so thin that it breaks extremely easily—handle with care.

3. Allow the gel medium to dry for 10 minutes. Then brush off excess leafing with a soft cloth or a soft brush. Save the excess for another project. Metal leaf should never be washed.

Save larger pieces of excess leafing to use again.

☀ **TIP**

Some leafings—both imitation and genuine gold and genuine silver—will tarnish with time. Imitation silver is actually aluminum and will not tarnish. Copper leafing is genuine and will patina. To prevent tarnish or patina, gently coat the leafing with a watered-down layer of gel medium.

Pearl Ex Powders

Pearl Ex is mica-based, acid-free, nontoxic, nontarnishing metallic or pearlescent pigments in powder form. These powders can be mixed into gutta and water-based resists, screen-printing inks, airbrush inks, fabric paints, oil or acrylic paints, gum arabic, or polymer clay. They can be mixed into a medium before applying or dusted, sprinkled, or rubbed onto a medium after applying while the medium is still wet. Use a foam or rubber stamp and gel medium to add a motif to fabric. Washing items with Pearl Ex will cause the powders to lose their luster, so it isn't recommended.

Variety of Pearl Ex Powdered Pigments

Supplies

- Jacquard Pearl Ex Powdered Pigments
- gel medium
- prewashed fabric
- foam or rubber stamps
- freezer paper or low-tack tape
- small paintbrushes
- polymer clay

MASKING

1. Mask off an area of your fabric with tape or a stencil cut from freezer paper.

Iron the freezer paper stencil to the background fabric.

2. Use a paintbrush and lightly apply a thin, even coat of gel medium to the masked area.

If more than one area is masked, apply medium to one area at a time to prevent drying before you add Pearl Ex.

3. Use a second, dry paintbrush to apply Pearl Ex onto the fresh gel medium. Repeat for multiple or larger masked areas. Before the gel medium dries, clean your brushes with water or water and soap.

Lightly touch the surface of the gel medium to prevent clogging your dry paintbrush.

Apply more gel medium and more Pearl Ex until the entire surface is covered.

Completed flower, with a second color applied to the center

STAMPING

1. Apply an even coat of gel medium to the stamp and press onto your fabric.

Because of the need for speed, a small stamp works best.

2. Working quickly, use a small paintbrush to dust Pearl Ex powder onto the fresh image. Before the medium dries, clean your brushes and rubber stamps with water and soap.

Because the entire motif is wet, you'll have to work fast before areas of it dry.

3. After 1 minute, brush off the excess Pearl Ex powder.

Completed image

POLYMER CLAY

1. Soften polymer clay by kneading it in your hands for several minutes. Form a small flat oval or round bead shape.

Using a wooden skewer, poke a hole in the bead for later attachment.

2. Press a rubber stamp into the surface of the clay bead to form an image in relief.

An allover textured stamp works well.

The clay will take the impression of the stamp.

3. Use your finger and lightly rub the Pearl Ex powder across the surface of the bead so that only the raised areas are covered. Follow the manufacturer's directions to bake the clay bead to harden.

Pick a matching or contrasting color of Pearl Ex.

Finished bead before baking

> ☀ **TRY THIS**
>
> ■ *Add Pearl Ex powders to paper pulp before pulling sheets of handmade paper.*
> ■ *Roll a polymer clay object in Pearl Ex prior to baking.*
> ■ *Lightly brush Pearl Ex across the surface of shrink film (see page 64) after coloring and before shrinking.*

Art Glitter

Use Art Glitter to add sparkle and pizazz to your projects, to fill in large areas, or to create fine detail. Glitter can be added before or after stitching. Once the fabric adhesive cures, the fabric is washable.

Art Glitters and Glue

Supplies

- Art Institute Glitter Microfine or Ultrafine Art Glitter
- Art Institute Glitter Fabric Dries Clear Adhesive
- prewashed fabric
- mechanical pencil
- fusible web (optional)
- small paintbrush
- foam brush
- foam or rubber stamp
- paper plate or cup
- freezer paper to iron to the back of your fabric for a more stable work surface (optional)

PAINTBRUSH APPLICATION

1. Lightly draw a design on the fabric with a mechanical pencil. Or cut out shapes of fabric with fusible web on the back and fuse to a background.

Dragonfly prepared for glitter

2. Use a small paintbrush to apply Fabric Dries Clear Adhesive to the fabric. Fill in just a small area, because the adhesive dries quickly.

Matching the color of the glitter to the appliqué fabric means that small missed areas won't be as obvious.

3. Pour a small amount of glitter onto the wet adhesive.

A little bit goes a long way!

Add more adhesive and more glitter to cover one area.

Shake the fabric gently for even coverage.

4. After a minute, shake the excess glitter onto a paper plate or into a paper cup. Add more adhesive and repeat until you have covered the entire area. When you are finished, return the unused glitter to the original container.

Completed glitter dragonfly

RUBBER STAMP APPLICATION

1. Use a foam brush to apply Fabric Dries Clear Adhesive to a rubber stamp. Stamp it onto the fabric.

Apply a fairly thick coat of adhesive to the stamp.

2. Pour a small amount of glitter onto the wet adhesive and shake the fabric gently for even coverage.

Work quickly to cover all the adhesive before it dries.

3. After a minute, shake the excess glitter onto a paper plate or into a paper cup. When you are finished, return the unused glitter to the original container.

4. Art Institute Glitter's Fabric Dries Clear Adhesive is heat settable. Not all adhesives can be rendered permanent and washable, so follow the manufacturer's instructions.

Completed stamped, glittered image

Flit, by Jane Dávila

☀ **TRY THIS**

- *Add glitter to the wings of insects, the scales of a fish, or dewdrops on a flower.*
- *Use white glitter to highlight areas of a snow-scene landscape.*
- *Use blue, green, or purple glitter on areas of water.*

Angelina Heat-Bondable Fiber

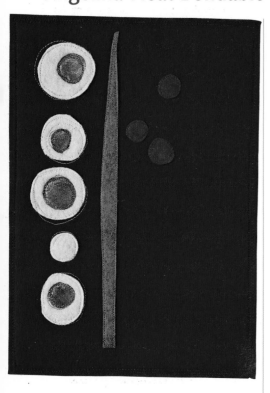

Angelina Heat-Bondable Fibers, as you might imagine, are fibers that when heated, melt and bond to each other creating a fabric-like sheet. The fibers bond only to each other and won't stick to other fibers. These fine, reflective, lustrous fibers have a soft hand and are available in several different styles and a large selection of colors. They are versatile and easy to use.

Bonded fiber sheets can be cut into shapes or used as is with rough, organic edges. They can be appliquéd onto a background or rolled, folded, or sculpted into three-dimensional design elements.

Supplies

- Angelina Heat-Bondable Fiber
- iron
- appliqué pressing sheet or parchment paper
- scissors

PROCEDURE

1. Place an appliqué pressing sheet or a piece of parchment paper on your ironing board.

2. Spread a small amount of Angelina fibers on the ironing surface.

3. Cover the fibers with another pressing sheet or parchment paper.

4. Press with an iron set to the silk temperature setting. Move the iron across the surface for a few seconds to create a sheet of fibers. Lift the iron and check the fibers to see whether they have bonded. If not, cover and press again for a few seconds, taking care not to overheat the fibers to prevent them from frying and losing their luster.

Bond the fibers by pressing.

The fibers will bond and form a sheet.

5. Once the fibers have bonded into a sheet, cut it into desired shapes and attach it to a background fabric with hand or machine stitching.

> **NOTE**
> *Pressing the fibers once they've bonded into a sheet, or using fusible web to attach the sheet, will alter the color of the fibers and diminish their luster.*

Lupe, by Elin Waterston

ANGELINA BEADS

1. Cut a small square from a bonded sheet of Angelina.

2. Carefully roll the square onto a skewer.

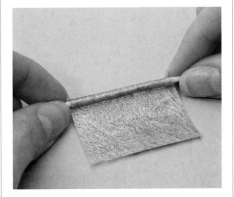

3. When the sheet is entirely rolled onto the skewer, cover with parchment paper and fuse the edge with an iron.

Beads made with sheets of Angelina

✸ TRY THIS

- *Add inclusions: Sandwich some sequins or snips of fabric or threads into the fibers before bonding. Be sure to heat test the inclusions first to make sure they won't melt.*
- *Emboss a sheet of Angelina: Place fibers over a rubber stamp, cover with parchment paper, and press.*
- *Experiment with thick and thin areas of the Angelina fibers.*
- *Combine two or more colors of Angelina.*

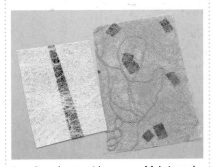

Angelina sheets with scraps of fabric and embroidery thread sandwiched between layers of fibers

CHAPTER THREE

STUDENT GALLERY

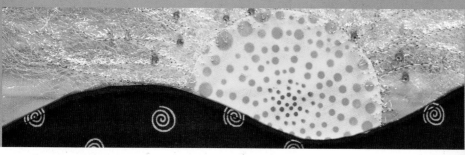

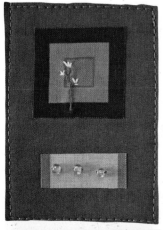

Artist Trading Cards, by Gretta Reed

The Climbing Tree, by Gail Ellspermann

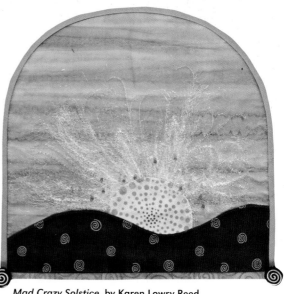

Mad Crazy Solstice, by Karen Lowry Reed

Love Is ... , by Cindy Silverstein

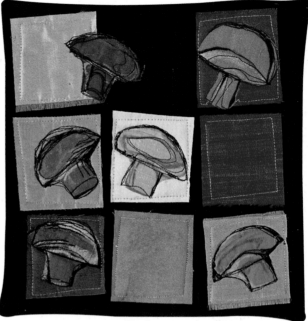

Champignons, by Carolyn Spiegel

Postcard, by Jacqueline Johnson

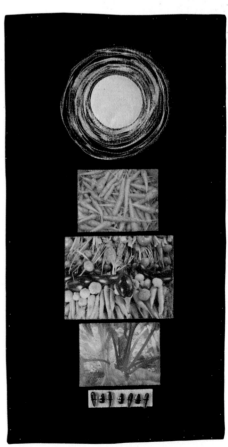

Harvest Moon, by Karen Lowry Reed

The Geisha, by Raquel McKinnon

Green Grid, by Gail Ellspermann

Gingko Flurry, by Norma Schlager

Kimono Room, by Selina Plotkin

CHAPTER **FOUR:**
CHALLENGES

"I must see new things and investigate them. I want to taste dark water and see crackling trees and wild wind." —Egon Schiele

challenge—(n.) a call or summons to engage in a contest, as of skill, strength, special effort, etc. (from Middle English: *chalenge*)

A challenge is an invitation to artists to create a work in response to or within a set of guidelines. Participating in a challenge is an excellent way to stretch yourself artistically. Working within the constraints of size, orientation, materials, deadlines, or themes can push you to work outside your comfort zone. A challenge can also provide inspiration to get you out of a creative slump.

To issue a challenge, choose a set of guidelines and regulations. Determine whether the challenge will require the use of certain materials or techniques and decide whether the participants will follow a set theme or choose their own. Establish size and orientation requirements as well as the deadline for projects to be completed.

I Say Tomahto,
by Elin Waterston,
quilt made for a word-
based challenge

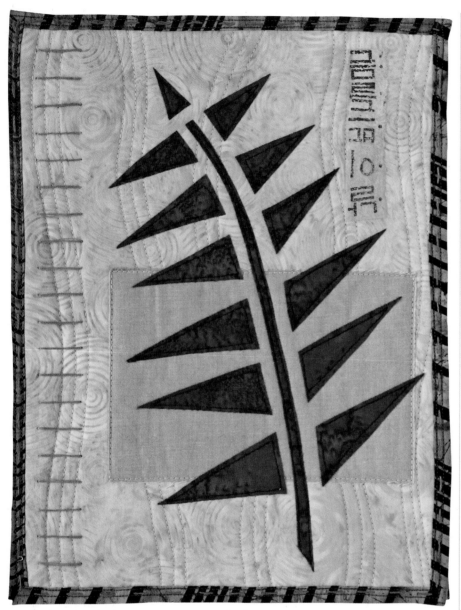

Abstract Fern, by Jane Dávila, quilt made for a challenge to abstract a photo

space, *childhood*, or *superstitions* are examples of broad subjects that can be interpreted many ways. Or a challenge may have a more specific topic, like *the moon, hopscotch,* or *black cats.* Participants may choose to interpret the subject literally or not so literally, or even quite abstractly or allegorically. Doing a little bit of research on a chosen subject will open up even more possibilities for directions to explore.

WORD CHALLENGES

Challenges based on words are particularly appealing. The translation of the written to the visual is open to many interpretations and can get the creative juices flowing. Each participant can work from the same phrase or poem, or each can be assigned (or choose) their own. Other ideas include basing a challenge on song lyrics, stories, or randomly chosen text (the third sentence on page 135 of any book, for example). Participants can simply open the dictionary and point to a word at random to use for the basis of a challenge, or they can write a selection of words on little slips of paper, place them in a basket, and choose at random.

☀ TRY THIS

Take your inspiration from fortune cookie fortunes, consecutive lines of a poem, sayings, platitudes (e.g., "every dog has his day"), or advertising slogans.

◉ NOTE

Remember not to incorporate any copyrighted lyrics or text into your piece without permission. However, using lyrics and text for inspiration is okay.

Challenge Themes

Some common starting points for a challenge include conceptual themes, such as specific subjects or words and phrases, or process-based themes that require specific materials, techniques, shapes, or sizes. A combination of these basic components can make for an interesting challenge. For example, a challenge might require the participants to base a challenge piece on a quote and incorporate a specific technique. Challenges can be very open with few restrictions or more defined with many rules. Either way, setting a theme can create a unifying element for the challenge pieces, while still allowing participants to explore and develop their works.

SUBJECT CHALLENGES

A challenge subject can offer a broad range of interpretation in which a multitude of ideas may immediately spring to mind. *Outer*

PROCESS CHALLENGES

A challenge might require the finished piece to be an atypical shape, such as a triangle, a circle, or a trapezoid. Specific materials and techniques can be the basis of a challenge in which every participant must use metallic paint or image transfer techniques. A requirement that challenges participants to think outside of what's expected or normal—for example, the incorporation of something found in a hardware store—can shake things up and produce interesting results.

The Artists

Some challenges are issued to a small number of select artists, whereas others are open calls for entry for actual or virtual exhibits. Groups or artist guilds often offer information about upcoming challenges. An Internet search for "art quilt challenge" will turn up quite a few items at any given time. In addition, many art publications, like *Quilting Arts Magazine* and *Cloth Paper Scissors*, list them as well.

If you have a gallery space or website to host an exhibit or a meeting place where members of a group are able to exhibit or share their finished pieces, you can set up your own challenge. Decide on a theme or set of regulations, including deadlines, and send out a call for entries. If your exhibit is planned for the Internet, you will need to include formatting instructions for the images, including file size, image size, resolution, and file type. Allow and encourage questions at the beginning of your challenge. Periodically check in with your participants to keep up their enthusiasm and to help them stay on track for the deadline.

The Projects

SUBJECT BASED: *LETTERS AND NUMBERS*

Jane issued a challenge to four artists to create a small art quilt (8″ × 10″), either vertical or horizontal orientation, with the subject *letters and numbers*. Each artist participating could interpret the theme with the techniques and materials of his or her choice.

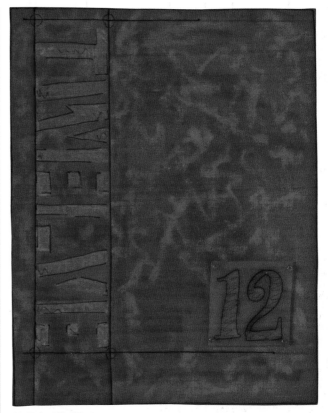

12.12, by Elin Waterston

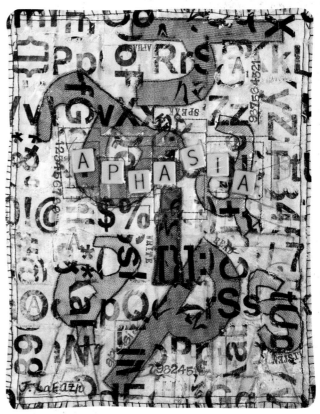

Aphasia, by Jane LaFazio

Safety in Numbers, by Jane Dávila

Red Letter Day, by Liz Berg

PHRASE BASED:
GAS FOOD LODGING

Elin based a challenge on the phrase *gas food lodging*. She invited four artists to make a small art quilt, no larger than 14″ on any side in any shape or orientation. The artists were free to use any techniques and materials they wished and were encouraged to make the pieces reflect their personal style.

Route 66, by Beryl Taylor

by wheatfields & watertowers, by Jane Dávila

Let's Eat, by Elin Waterston

gas food lodging, by Tricia McKellar

"Every artist dips his brush in his own soul, and paints his own nature into his pictures." —Henry Ward Beecher

collaborate—(v.) to work together, especially in a joint intellectual effort (from Latin *laborare*: to work)

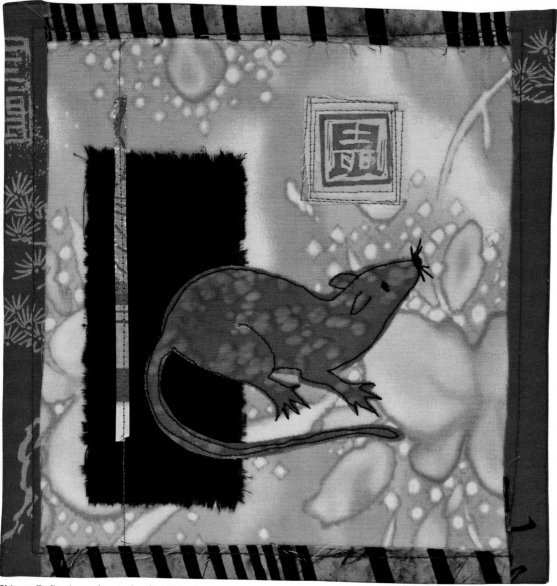

Chinese Zodiac journal page, by Elin Waterston

Collaborations, or projects done with other artists, can be a good way to stretch yourself and explore themes and techniques you might not otherwise attempt. Collaborations can be held between artists who know each other (in the real world or in cyberspace) or artists who don't know each other yet but would like to work together. The process of collaborating can be a growth experience—artists must adjust to other people's working styles; deal with expectations, deadlines, compromise, and inspiration; and can push the participating artists outside their comfort zones. Each artist's personal work will benefit from this exposure to a collaborating group of artists.

Certain things need to be decided at the start of a collaboration: the size of the group (large or small, invited or open); time constraints (length of project, duration of passing time, deadlines); type of project; dispute resolution (timeliness, drop-outs, participants who don't follow the rules); communication (frequency and method); media (textile only or include other media); moderator (who/his or her responsibilities); confidentiality (do the participants share their work with each other while the project is ongoing or is the work revealed when the project is complete?); and whether to end up with one piece total or one piece per artist.

The group must agree up front on the objectives of the project. Even though each artist may be looking to get something different out of a project, the group as a whole should agree on some basic guidelines. Everyone must agree to abide by time constraints, to finish the project, and to follow the rules as decided upon by the group. It is also imperative that each artist understands the need to work to the best of his or her ability and to take the commitment seriously.

If group members are located at a distance from each other, it will be necessary to mail or ship projects back and forth. These shipping costs and the decision of a method of shipment should be taken into consideration. Some artists might choose to include a small notebook or journal with a project so that contributing artists can write down thoughts, ideas, explanations, and inspirations. Completed pieces should be signed and labeled with name, date, location, and a brief description of the project.

Chinese Zodiac journal page, by Kathryn Hunter

Madame Fortuna, shrine by Janet Ghio

The Artists

A collaboration has a minimum of two artists and no set maximum. The size of the group and the amount of time available can determine which type of collaborative project to choose. With some projects (i.e., those that travel to each member of the group), the larger the group, the longer the time frame will need to be. With others (like a surprise package project), the number of "players" is immaterial to the time frame; instead it depends heavily on the moderator. Any collaboration with three or more artists should have a moderator. The moderator's job is to disseminate information, keep everyone on track, and negotiate problems or disputes.

Another consideration when setting up a collaborative group is the relative skill level of the members. Although it might seem more advantageous to work within a group of peers who are all at a similar level of technical and artistic ability, there can be rewards to working with a group of mixed levels. For those farther along in their artistic development, the opportunity to collaborate with those artists discovering their creative abilities can be gratifying and enriching. Beginning artists exposed to more experienced artists will find themselves pushed and inspired.

If you already belong to a group of artists who meet on a regular basis (e.g., a guild or artists' association), you can issue an open call for a collaborative project, closing it when an optimal number of members is reached or by a specific deadline. If you wish to work with a specific group of artists, compose a letter of invitation that details everything about the project, from concept to deadlines. Do not be discouraged if everyone does not respond affirmatively; just be prepared to ask other artists.

Communication is an important component to a successful collaboration. In-person gatherings and exchanges work well when everyone is located geographically close together, especially if a collaborative project grows out of a local group that already meets on a regular basis. An alternative is to communicate via email. You can set up an address "group" in your email program so that you can send messages to the entire group with one address. Or you can form an online group and open the membership only to the participants of your collaboration. The advantage of an online group is that many sites provide a secure place to store group information (such as mailing addresses), hold polls for things being decided upon, and share photos of work in progress.

Chinese Zodiac journal cover, by Elin Waterston

The Projects

FABRIC ART JOURNALS

Each artist participating in a fabric art journal collaboration creates a cover that determines the color scheme, theme, size, and orientation (vertical or horizontal) for his or her journal. The project moderator determines a traveling order. Each contributing artist creates a page for each journal. The pages are passed in turn to each of the participating artists, ultimately returning to the originating artist, who makes a back cover and binds the pages into a book.

Journal pages can be created as two independently designed pages or as a two-sided unit. Two-sided pages require planning so that elements and stitching from one side make sense on the other. Another thing to consider is how your design relates to the preceding page.

Pages can be built on a heavy interfacing like Timtex or fast2fuse, thin batting, or heavy fabric or paper. Page edges can be bound, pinked, topstitched, satin stitched, painted, or couched with a thick yarn.

Chinese Zodiac pages,
by Kathryn Hunter (L) and Jane LaFazio (R)

Chinese Zodiac pages,
by Woodie Anderson (L) and Elin Waterston (R)

SURPRISE PACKAGE

Each participating artist collects an assortment of stuff in a quart or gallon resealable bag. The moderator determines the size of the bag before the start of the project so that each artist contributes roughly the same amount of stuff. The bags are collected by the moderator and randomly exchanged, without either the receiving artist or the originating artist knowing who has which bag. The moderator keeps records or a master list of the exchange, as well as photos of the contents of every bag. This enables all the participants to see the materials each artist had to work with at the beginning.

The receiving artist must make an art quilt within the parameters of size, orientation, time limit, and other agreed-upon guidelines. Variations include using all or most of the bag contents; adding outside elements of fabric and embellishments, or not allowing outside elements; working within a theme; or letting each artist choose his or her own subject. This is a one-to-one exchange; that is, one artist makes one quilt for one other artist. This type of collaboration is especially good for larger groups. A moderator is absolutely essential for a project of this nature.

Some ideas for contents are unusual or specialty fabrics; found objects; embellishments like beads, sequins, and charms; and fun fibers and threads. If the group includes artists in more than one country, it will be necessary to restrict the contents of the bags due to customs regulations. For international exchanges, do not include any plant or animal material like seeds, leaves, feathers, bones, or shells, as the bag will be delayed at customs and might be destroyed. Also, if the group includes individuals with allergies or other sensitivities, it may be advisable to have a pet-free or smoke-free subgroup.

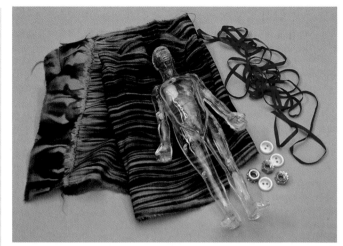

Original contents of a surprise package quilt, sent by Tricia McKellar

Original contents of a surprise package quilt, sent by Karen Stiehl Osborn

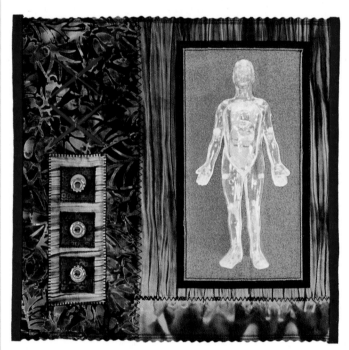

Man Enough, by Jane Dávila; completed surprise package quilt

Night Garden, by Janet Ghio; completed surprise package quilt

Original contents of a surprise package quilt, sent by Jane Dávila

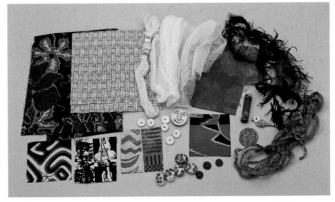

Original contents of a surprise package quilt, sent by Janet Ghio

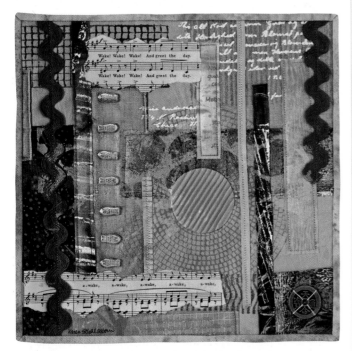

Morning Song, by Karen Stiehl Osborn; completed surprise package quilt

Nest, by Tricia McKellar; completed surprise package quilt

✳ TIP

If you receive an item that presents a challenge, think outside the box to come up with a creative way to use it.

EXQUISITE CORPSE

This form of collaboration—a collective collage of images (or words) called an exquisite corpse—began as a Surrealist game. In a traditional exquisite corpse, a picture is developed, with each artist working from a small visible section of the image contributed by the previous artist. As it has come to be used among quilt artists, an image (usually a photograph) is chosen and sliced into pieces. Each artist receives a segment of the photo and recreates that segment following the guidelines and size specifications set up by the project's moderator. The segments can be hung together or attached to each other to replicate the original image.

Photos that contain interesting elements in each section work well for this project. The photos can be sliced into long vertical or horizontal pieces or into equal or unequal squares or rectangles.

Original photo of flowers

Original street scene photo

Flowers photo divided into segments

Street scene photo divided into segments

> ⊙ **NOTE**
>
> Use only copyright-free photographs and images, photos that you've taken, or photos that you have permission from the photographer to use. Elin's husband, David, took the photos that we used for our projects. We asked nicely, and he gave us permission!

Mille Fiori, **finished quilt with segments by Liz Berg, Terry Grant, and Jane Dávila**

Trippin, finished quilt with segments by Jane LaFazio, Kathryn Hunter, and Elin Waterston

Depending on the size of the finished pieces and the shape of the slices, you will be confronted with creative opportunities for reassembling the segments into one piece. Long vertical slices can simply be hung next to each other on one rod, assuming that all the pieces have a sleeve attached at the same height. Squares or rectangles can be hand-tacked to each other and hung as one unit or left separate and hung as individual pieces. It should be determined at the beginning of the project whether there will be consensus for edge finishing.

MIXED MEDIA ART

Another project to consider is a mixed media collaboration, in which the participants must use an element or found object given to them by another participant. Choose an unusual form (like an odd shape or something three-dimensional) or include an unusual technique or material in the list of requirements. You need not limit the number of participants, though it is difficult to add artists once the project has started.

We chose to have our participants create a freestanding, three-dimensional shrine that was between 5″ and 8″ tall. Jane, acting as moderator, created a mailing list with all the names and addresses of the players. Each participating artist sent a found object to another artist on the list. The found objects had to be used in the shrine but could be altered in any way. One thing to ask everyone to keep in mind when choosing found objects for a project like this is the size of the finished work. A very large or very small found object would be difficult or impossible to incorporate into these shrines.

TIP

Just before beginning the project, circulate a list with everyone's names and addresses. Have every artist confirm the spelling and accuracy of mailing addresses to avoid potential problems.

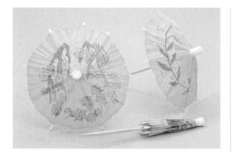

Found object: paper drink umbrellas

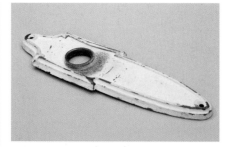

Found object: antique door plate

Found object: antique spoon

Beautiful Flower by Gail Ellspermann

Wings to Fly, by Jane Dávila

Let Me Feed Your Soul, by Kim Rae Nugent

Found object: lens from vintage sunglasses

Madame Fortuna, by Janet Ghio

Found object: metal candle drip holder

Found object: face bead

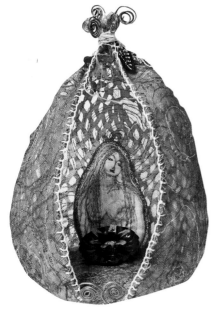

Crimson Little Flower, by Natalya Aikens

cielo, by Elin Waterston

☀ TRY THIS

Possible projects:

■ *Three-dimensional art, such as fabric boxes, bowls, or vessels*

■ *Wearable art bags*

■ *Cloth art dolls*

■ *Collages combining textiles with other media, such as polymer clay, wax encaustic, watercolor, or paper*

Try variations on the listed projects:

■ *Make an accordion book or make "pages" but display them creatively—for example, in an altered art box, attached to a larger quilt, in frames, or on unusually shaped pages.*

■ *Send interesting fabric or embellishments to each other.*

■ *Choose a monochromatic color palette to work in or begin inspiration with an assigned word.*

■ *Divide a photo into squares, rectangles, or trapezoids instead of slices.*

CHAPTER SIX:

ART TO TRADE

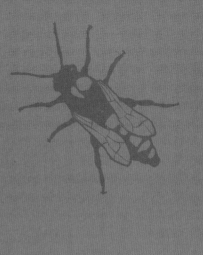

> "An artist is someone who produces things that people don't need to have but that he, for some reason, thinks it would be a good idea to give them."
>
> —Andy Warhol

exchange—(v.) to give in return for something equivalent (from Middle English: *eschaungen*)

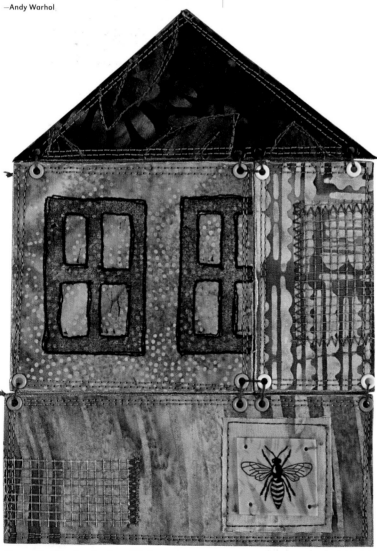

Domestic Affection, by Jane Dávila

Creating art to trade with other artists can be a fun way to explore new techniques, to stretch yourself artistically, and to build up your art collection. There are many online groups for swapping Fiber Art Postcards and Artist Trading Cards. With group swaps, each artist swaps a set number of pieces with other members of the group. You can join an existing group or set one up yourself. Art can also be swapped one on one. Contact an artist whose work you admire and suggest a trade; be open to a trade if someone contacts you.

If you'd like to set up your own swap, some of the things you'll need to keep in mind are the time frame for completion, the size of the finished art (unless you're swapping postcards or Artist Trading Cards, which have predetermined sizes), the method of exchange (by mail or in person), and the number of participants. It is usually helpful for one person to act as a moderator. The job of moderator can be assigned to another member if the group decides to continue and do multiple swaps.

If you join a swap, it is important to realize that you are making a commitment. Every artist entering a swap is acknowledging an obligation to send out the required pieces in a timely fashion. It is very bad form to join a swap, receive art, and not reciprocate.

ARTIST TRADING CARDS

Artist Trading Cards, by Elin Waterston

Artist Trading Cards (or ATCs) are just what they sound like—cards that are traded among artists. ATCs are 2½″ × 3½″, the size of commercial trading cards, baseball cards, and standard playing cards. Cards can be built on any support, such as cardstock, watercolor paper, heavy interfacing like fast2fuse, or commercial trading or playing cards. Cards are often made for a specific swap in which a moderator or host sets up guidelines for all participants.

Depending on the rules of the swap, artists are usually free to use the methods and materials of their choice. Typically cards are flat and vertical in orientation, as that is what works best for the most common display methods. Although some swaps allow prints or copies of a single design, each card is usually an original work of art. Many artists often create a series of similar cards.

Some artists create a large background fabric—for example, by painting, stamping, dyeing, collaging, or sewing. The background fabric can be built directly on the support material, cut into 2½″ × 3½″ pieces, and used as a base for other elements. Other artists approach each card individually, creating tiny compositions one at a time.

Circus theme ATCs, by Woodie Anderson

Circus theme ATCs, by Andrea C. Jenkins

Circus theme ATCs, by Mati Rose McDonough

Many swaps happen through the mail. Each artist mails a set number of cards. Transparent trading card sleeves have nine pockets, so swaps are often done as nine for nine or perhaps eight for eight, in which the artist makes nine but keeps one of his or her own to complete the set. Once all the cards are received, the host shuffles the cards and sends back the same number of cards each artist has sent. Thus, in a nine-card swap, each artist sends nine cards and gets nine cards—one each from nine different artists. Many swappers include an extra card as a gift for the host. Swaps can also be done in person at swap meets, where artists gather and make one-on-one trades with other artists. Both methods are a way to meet and network with other artists, get ideas, learn new methods, and build your ATC collection.

There is an understanding among ATC artists that cards are never to be sold, only traded with other artists. Recently some artists have begun producing Art Card Editions and Originals (or ACEOs) that can be traded or sold. But it is not about the money! The fun of ATCs and ACEOs is in creating and collecting miniature art and becoming part of an artistic community, whether it's virtual or actual.

To organize and host a swap, gather names and addresses of participants and set up guidelines, including theme, number of cards, deadlines, and other regulations. Once you have received all the cards, shuffle them and send them back out to all the swappers, making certain that everyone gets a card from different artists. Remember to have each swapper include a self-addressed stamped envelope (SASE) with his or her cards.

Set of circus-themed Artist Trading Cards, by (top row L–R) Elin Waterston, Woodie Anderson, Andrea C. Jenkins; (middle row L–R) Mati Rose McDonough, Natalya Aikens, Kathryn Hunter; (bottom row L–R) Gail Ellspermann, Jane Dávila, Jane LaFazio

❋ TRY THIS

Create an interesting container to house or display the cards once received.

FIBER ART POSTCARDS

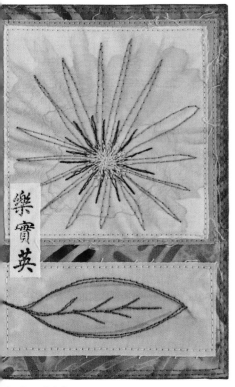

by Jane Dávila

Ancient Courses of the Mississippi,
by Kathryn Hunter

Fiber Art Postcards are small pieces of art intended to be sent through the mail without envelopes. The postcards are 4″ × 6″ and are usually less than ⅛″ thick. They can be oriented either vertically or horizontally, although the majority of them tend to be horizontal. Postcards can be constructed on heavy interfacing like fast2fuse, thin batting, or watercolor paper. Usually the face of a postcard is completed—all fusing, sewing, and embellishing—before the address side is attached.

Edges can be finished by couching yarn or ribbon around the perimeter, satin stitching over the raw edge, topstitching, binding, facing, or hand embroidering. Try to keep any embellishments fairly light and flat. Although the postcards might be hand cancelled at the post office, they will travel through sorting machines at some point in their journey, so be certain that everything is attached securely. The stamp counts too, so look for a cool one!

Time is a Jewel Without Replacement,
by Kim Rae Nugent

Postcards can be created following a theme and can have requirements of color, orientation, or technique—or not. (The postcards pictured are based on the theme *Time.*) Every participant makes a postcard for every other participant. A mailing list is created and distributed so participants can send their cards to other participants. Postcards need to be completed and mailed within the time frame determined either by the moderator or by vote from the group.

Zoom, by Elin Waterston

Always on Time, by Andrea C. Jenkins

The 25th Hour, by Gail Ellspermann

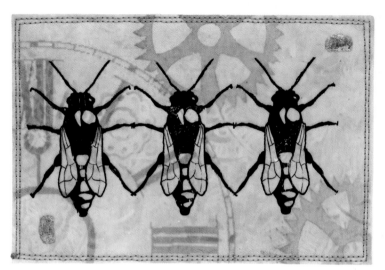

Time Flies, by Jane Dávila

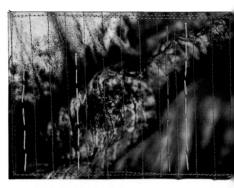

Time, by Tricia McKellar

Create an address side for the post-card either by printing on fabric directly from your computer or by hand lettering on a light-colored fabric. Keep the address side background fairly light in color so the postal service's address-reading machines can read it easily. A simple and fast alternative is to print out address label stickers to adhere to the back of the postcard. A piece of heavy cardstock can be used for the address side instead of fabric.

Take the finished cards to the post office to purchase postage. Regular first-class postage is usually sufficient, but a thick or heavy postcard may require more. Rub self-adhesive stamps in place vigorously to ensure a good seal.

Memories, by Karen Stiehl Osborn

Address side of postcards

Bedtime, by Terry Grant

RockTreeSky—Mother Nature's Time, by Virginia A. Spiegel

✳ TIP

If your postcard incorporates anything very delicate, consider applying a layer of gel medium or an acrylic finish to increase its sturdiness.

☀ TRY THIS

Some fun topics to try are recycled items, embellishments, elements of design, inspiring words, or obscure holidays.

✳ TIP

If you are sending postcards out of the country, do not use any organic or plant materials in their construction, as they will most likely be discarded in customs.

Mail your cards and wait to see what appears in your mailbox!

SMALL ART SWAPS

house:home quilt, by Tricia McKellar

In addition to ATC and postcard swaps, small works of art can also be traded. Depending on the number of participants in the group, a swap can be set up so each participant gets a piece from every other artist. If the group is too large for each artist to make one piece for every participant, the moderator can decide on a set number of pieces that each artist makes, or he or she can randomly shuffle names so that each player makes just one piece and receives just one piece. Whether each artist makes one piece or many pieces, each artist receives the same number of pieces he or she has made and sent.

As with other swaps, the moderator sets the rules and regulations, determines deadlines, and establishes mailing instructions. Small art swaps can be theme based or open themed and can have a set size or a minimum and maximum range. The moderator can also include some requirement, such as the use of a specific fabric, technique, or color. Although each work made for a swap can be a complete original, pieces can also be made as a series with variations.

black bird swap quilts, by Beryl Taylor; each work is unique.

black bird swap quilts, by Woodie Anderson; a series of similar works

For Jane's small art swap, the six participating artists were invited to make six small quilts, each 5″ × 7″ in a vertical orientation. The theme of the swap was *house: home*, which the artists could interpret in any way they chose, using any techniques or materials they desired. Some of the artists chose to create quilts that aren't rectangles but that still fit within the size limitations. Each artist received one work from every other artist.

If you are trading art one on one, it can be fun to think about the presentation of the finished swap piece. For example, Virginia Spiegel put a lot of creativity into packaging her swap piece. It is a work of art even before the lucky recipient opens it!

house:home swap quilts, by (top row L–R) Jane Dávila, Liz Berg, Natalya Aiken; (bottom row L–R) Karen Stiehl Osborn, Tricia McKellar, Terry Grant

For Elin's small art swap, each of the nine participating artists was asked to make nine 6″ × 6″ quilts with a *black bird* theme. The artists were free to interpret the theme as loosely or literally as they wanted and to use the methods or techniques of their choice. No sleeves or hanging devices were requested so that the swappers could decide how to display the finished quilts—either assembled into one large piece or hung as independent pieces.

※ TRY THIS

At the conclusion of the swap, have participants share the ways they displayed or assembled the pieces.

black bird swap quilts, by (top row L–R) Elin Waterston, Janet Ghio, Kathryn Hunter; (middle row L–R) Woodie Anderson, Beryl Taylor, Jane LaFazio; (bottom row L–R) Virginia A. Spiegel, Gail Ellspermann, Rayna Gillman

CHAPTER SEVEN

CONNECTIONS

"Art is not made for anybody and is, at the same time, for everybody." —**Piet Mondrian**

connect—(v.) to join, unite, or link; to associate or establish communication between (from late Middle English: *connectere*)

ONLINE GROUPS AND THE INTERNET

The Internet has given us the ability to communicate with people in nearly every corner of the world. We are able to reach out and instantly find people who share our interests. There are many existing groups of art quilters, textile, and mixed media artists on the Internet. A simple search will turn up many of them. Some of these are closed to new members, have waiting lists, or require an application process; however, the majority are very welcoming to fresh faces.

Alternatively, you can start your own Internet group. Take a look at a few groups to see what appeals to you and model your group after the attributes you like best. The fastest and easiest way to set up a group is on the Yahoo! Groups website.

la primavera, by Jane Dávila

Pájaros Rosados, **by Jane Dávila**

Groups at this site have the ability to load files, create databases and polls, post photographs, and, of course, send messages. Yahoo! Groups can be open or closed, and sending invitations or promoting a group is simple. Visit **groups.yahoo.com** for more information.

Another way to communicate with other artists is by starting a blog (short for web log). Blogs are online journals where people post entries and photographs and invite comments from readers. Blogs are more interactive and immediate than standard websites. Many blog servers provide free service. Other blog servers can be added to your existing website or may require a monthly or yearly fee. It's simple to create a blog. Most servers have customizable templates to get you started. A digital camera and a scanner can be very helpful to add visual content to your blog.

Promote your blog by listing the address on your business cards, in your email signature line, and in online groups. Blogs that aren't updated regularly aren't visited often, so try to post something new at least once a week. Leave comments on other blogs so that people will follow you back to your blog to learn more about you. List the blogs that you like to read in the sidebar of your blog and ask others to do the same for you. A blog can be very personal and revealing or can be strictly focused on your art and artistic doings. It can also have the positive benefit of causing you to produce more art, just so you have something new to post. Blog rings are formed by linking blogs with a common theme together. Some of the most commonly used blog servers are **www.blogger.com**, **www.typepad.com**, and **www.wordpress.com**.

June & the Elephant, **by Elin Waterston**

SMALL IN-PERSON GROUPS

If you prefer to meet other artists in person, join a local group. Many art guilds and art centers have regular member meetings. Information about small groups can be found at these meetings and in guild newsletters. Meeting with a group of artists working in a variety of media—ceramics, fiber, water-colors, sculpture, oils, jewelry—can invigorate your art and present new opportunities for exhibitions and sales.

If you are unable to find a local group to suit your needs, start your own. Secure a meeting place—either someone's home or a commercial location—and adver-tise at art centers, guilds, and over the Internet. Although it might take time, if you keep at it, you'll end up with a group of like-minded artists with whom you can share ideas, support, and a sense of community.

> ⊚ **NOTE**
>
> *Some things to consider when starting a group: the meeting location; frequency of meetings; objective of the group—camara-derie, exhibiting, education; types of media—all fiber or a variety; size of the group; and an agenda.*

Pisces, by Elin Waterston

CRITIQUE GROUPS

A critique (crit) group is a group of artists who gather to view and discuss one another's work. If possible, join or start a group with artists at your level of expertise and experience. Critique groups can meet weekly or monthly; the number of pieces reviewed can be decided upon prior to the meeting. Groups can have any number of members, though groups that are either very small or very large can be ineffective or unwieldy.

Critiques are serious, thoughtful discussions of style and technique in which members evaluate each other's work. Typically one artist presents work for the group's consideration. The group discusses whether the work is successful and what the artist can do to improve the work. A critique is not a criticism but rather a conversation exploring the varying approaches to common problems—the "whys" of art.

Keep in mind that a critique is an opinion. If many people share the same opinion about your work, it might be worthwhile to consider their suggestions. If the group holds varying opinions, heed the ones that make sense to you. A critique can also give the artist an opportunity to verbalize his or her thought processes, inspiration, and motivations regarding a piece of art or a series. This verbalization can be very helpful to an artist's development.

Although not every artist finds a critique group necessary or helpful, it can be an avenue to explore and to further artistic growth. One benefit of a critique group can be the fresh perspective to your work. Artists at every level in their career can find a critique group useful, but it isn't for everyone.

Pescado Salvaje, by Jane Dávila

❋ MORE IDEAS

■ *Join an online crit group.*

■ *Join or form a crit group for artists working in many different media.*

■ *Look for small break-off groups from larger national or international groups, such as the Studio Art Quilt Associates and the Surface Design Association.*

■ *Join or form an online group on the photo-sharing site* Flickr.com.

■ *Become a member of* deviantART.com *to connect with other artists, showcase your art, invite comments, and receive newsletters.*

CHAPTER EIGHT

COLLABORATING
ARTISTS GALLERY

house:home quilt, by Karen Stiehl Osborn

house:home quilt, by Liz Berg

house:home quilt, by Terry Grant

black bird quilt, by Janet Ghio

black bird quilt, by Virginia A. Spiegel

house:home quilt, by Natalya Aiken

black bird quilt, by Rayna Gillman

Journal page, by Mati Rose McDonough

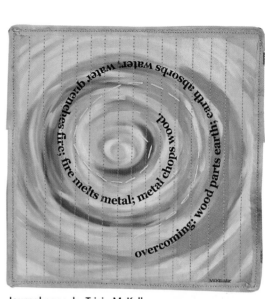

overcoming: wood parts earth; earth absorbs water; water quenches fire; fire melts metal; metal chops wood.

Journal page, by Tricia McKellar

Journal page, by Jane LaFazio

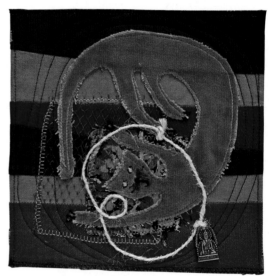

Journal page, by Woodie Anderson

Journal page, by Janet Ghio

Assembled journal

PARTICIPATING ARTISTS

NATALYA AIKENS

grew up in St. Petersburg, Russia, listening to her dad read Russian fairy tales to her and then reading them voraciously herself. Her art is an exploration of her heritage. Life has allowed her many ways to try her hand at art. In fiber art, she has found the way to meld her love of fabric, paint, and all things textural. Once again, fairy tales are filling her head with visions of magic, love, and heroism.

Website: www.artbynatalya.com
Blog: artbynatalya.blogspot.com

WOODIE ANDERSON

is an artist and designer living and working in Winston-Salem, North Carolina. Her mixed media serigraphs and three-dimensional fiber works have been described as focused, smart, and playful. Combining print making, fiber work, and graphic elements with found fabrics, collage, and stitching in her work, she explores a colorful world of word balloons, elasticized body parts, embryonic faces, and playful typography. Anderson is also a member of the artist collective SEED and a participating artist in the Art*o*mat.

Website: www.deftgurl.com
Email: woodie@deftgurl.com

LIZ BERG

spent her childhood moving around with her parents, as her father was in the Navy. This gave her the opportunity to live in Japan for four years and graduate from high school in Hawaii. Liz has always been interested in art, and her mother was an artist who encouraged her explorations. Liz majored in fine arts for the first two years of college, then switched to social welfare. Married after graduation, she went to work for the Alameda County Probation Department. In 1999, she retired as a probation officer and began her career as a full-time studio artist working in fiber and mixed media.

Website: www.lizbergartquilts.com
Blog: lizcreates.blogspot.com
Email: lizberg@sbcglobal.net

GAIL ELLSPERMANN

is a mixed media artist who began her creative career as a floral designer. Her love for color and texture evolved into an interest in collage and quilting, the primary focus of her work. When not in her studio, Gail can be found scouting flea markets and thrift stores in search of interesting items to use in her work. She has written several books for Design Originals, including the art doll book *Divine Divas*. Her work has appeared in *Somerset Studio* and *Quilting Arts Magazine*.

Website: www.GailHarteDesigns.com
Email: GailHarteDesigns@aol.com

JANET GHIO

is a contemporary, narrative fiber artist who has been making art quilts since 1996. Her quilts are the culmination of her life-long interest in different types of hand stitchery and fiber work. She is very interested in the textiles, images, symbols, and iconography of other cultures. She loves all types of embellishment, particularly beadwork. Many of her art quilts and three-dimensional pieces are tributes to the magic and mystery of women. She has written articles for *Quilting Arts Magazine* and has been featured in *Cloth Paper Scissors* magazine and other publications. Her work has been shown in many galleries around the country, as well as at numerous exhibits. Janet lives with her husband and her dog, Sparky, in Kerrville, Texas.

Website: www.quiltcollage.com
Email: jaghio11@ktc.com

RAYNA GILLMAN

works in mixed media on textiles and paper. She is a sought-after surface design teacher, noted for her intuitive sense of color and ability to infuse her workshops with a sense of play as she encourages students to experiment using the words *What if?* She has been featured on *Simply Quilts* and has written for *Quilting Arts Magazine*. Her work has appeared in the *Surface Design Journal*. Her award-winning art has been exhibited internationally and is in private collections in the United States, France, and Belgium.

Websites: www.studio78.net and www.galleryfxv.com
Blog: studio78notes.blogspot.com
Email: rgillman@studio78.net.

TERRY GRANT

was born in Colorado, grew up in Idaho, and has lived in Oregon since 1979. She has been making art quilts for more than 20 years. She has a Bachelor of Arts degree in art from Idaho State University and is a graphic designer. Her quilts have been exhibited at the International Quilt Festival in Houston, Texas; the International Quilt Expo in Lyons, France; the Association of Pacific Northwest Quilts in Seattle, Washington; and other national and regional shows. She has had work published in *Quilters Newsletter Magazine*, *Quiltmaker* magazine, and two books.

Blog: andsewitgoes.blogspot.com
Email: terry.grant@comcast.net

KATHRYN HUNTER

is a mixed media artist and printmaker. She currently teaches visual art foundations at the University of Louisiana, Lafayette. She also runs a custom letterpress printing business, Blackbird Letterpress.

Websites: www.blackbirdletterpress.com and
             blackbirdletterpress.etsy.com
Email: blackbirdletterpress@yahoo.com

ANDREA C. JENKINS

is a woman who likes to cut and paste things. She also likes to play around with words and movement and is quite handy with the camera. Andrea currently lives in Portland, Oregon, with her husband, Ward, and two children, Ava and Ezra. She also bakes a mean red velvet cake.

Blog: hulaseventy.blogspot.com

JANE LAFAZIO

is a mixed media artist who works in paper and cloth. She began teaching her popular Art Quilt Explorations class in 2005 (now online through **joggles.com**). She also teaches mixed media and watercolor journaling classes and workshops. Her artwork has been featured in *Material Visions: A Gallery of Miniature Art Quilts*, *Fabric Art Gallery*, *Beginner's Guide to Art Quilts*, and Danny Gregory's *An Illustrated Life*, as well as in *Cloth Paper Scissors* and *Quilting Arts Magazine*. Jane also has an instructional DVD entitled *The Small Art Quilt*.

Website: www.plainjanestudio.com
Blog: janeville.blogspot.com
Email: jane@plainjanestudio.com

MATI ROSE MCDONOUGH

is 31, but paints like a sophisticated child. It has taken years for Mati to get to this place of freedom, even though she has gone to two schools to study fine art and painting—namely, Macalester College and the California College of the Arts. She has had numerous shows, has published several illustrations, and hopes that this is just the beginning. Along with her talented husband, Hugh D'Andrade, she makes messes and daily discoveries in her studio behind her home called Compound 21.

Websites: www.matirose.com and suspectshoppe.etsy.com
Blog: matirose.blogspot.com
Email: matimcd@hotmail.com

TRICIA MCKELLAR

is a mixed media artist in North Carolina. Her works often wrestle with the themes, How does all the stuff of our lives fit together? Is it a neat equation? How do chance and chaos contribute to our circumstance? Each work is an exploration of another permutation, another tangle of objects.

Website: www.triciamckellar.com
Blog: triciamckellar.com/note99
Email: tm@triciamckellar.com

KIM RAE NUGENT

is an artist and author from rural Wisconsin. She enjoys sharing her passion of the creative process through her art featured in numerous publications. She has spent her life cultivating skills in mixed media, including collage, sewing, altered books, and assemblage. Kim's love of nature, especially animals, is often reflected in her art.

Websites: www.kimraenugent.com and
             www.raevns-nest-art-retreat.com
Blog: kimraenugent.blogspot.com
Email: kimnugent@yahoo.com

KAREN STIEHL OSBORN

is a dynamic textile and mixed media artist. She is best known for her bold use of vibrant colors and her abstract, collage style. Karen's work has appeared in publications, exhibitions, and galleries around the world, and she has work in private and museum collections in the United States, Belgium, Germany, the United Kingdom, Mexico, and New Zealand.

Website: www.KarenStiehlOsborn.com
Email: Karen@KarenStiehlOsborn.com

VIRGINIA A. SPIEGEL

makes textile and mixed media art. Her artwork is held in private and public collections throughout the world. She shares her interests and inspirations in her ongoing online book, *Art, Nature, Creativity, Life*. Virginia is the founder of Fiberart For A Cause, fund-raising for the American Cancer Society.

Website: www.virginiaspiegel.com
Blog: virginiaspiegel.com/blog
Email: virginia@virginiaspiegel.com

BERYL TAYLOR

arrived in the United States in 2002 from England, having graduated in City and Guilds Creative Embroidery. While in Britain, she spent many years exhibiting her work with a textile group called Threadmill. She also taught many workshops in mixed media collage. Since arriving in the United States, Beryl has continued to teach workshops. Her work has been published in many national and international magazines, and she exhibits her work both in the United States and throughout the world. In June 2006, her first book, *Mixed Media Explorations*, was published.

Website: www.beryltaylor.com
Email: berylptaylor@aol.com

INDEX

Enso: high in the haze, by Elin Waterston

Temps, **by Jane Dávila**

FLOURISH!
Country Quilter
344 Route 100
Somers, NY 10589
888-277-7780
www.countryquilter.com

Comprehensive mail order and retail art quilting supplies, fabric, fibers, books, paint, ink, stamp pads, beads, ink-jet fabrics, resists, tools

DHARMA TRADING
800-542-5227
www.dharmatrading.com
Mail order surface design supplies

BLICK ART MATERIALS
800-828-4548
www.dickblick.com
Mail order art and craft supplies

PEARL PAINT
800-451-7327
www.pearlpaint.com
Mail order art supplies

JERRY'S ARTARAMA
www.jerrysartarama.com
Mail order art supplies

PRO CHEMICAL
PRO Chemical & Dye
P.O. Box 14
Somerset, MA 02726
800-228-9393
www.prochemical.com
Mail order paints and dyes

NASCO ARTWORKS
800-558-9595
www.enasco.com/artsandcrafts
Mail order art and craft supplies

ST. THERESA TEXTILE TROVE
5846 Hamilton Avenue
Cincinnati, OH 45224
800-236-2450
www.sttheresatextile.com
Unique fabric and embellishments

QUILTING ARTS
23 Gleasondale Road
Stow, MA 01775-1319
www.quiltingarts.com
1-866-698-6989
Books, magazines, surface design supplies

SPEEDBALL ART PRODUCTS
800-898-7224
www.speedballart.com
Printmaking and stamp making supplies

FAIRFIELD PROCESSING
800-980-8000
www.poly-fil.com
Batting

JACQUARD PRODUCTS
800-442-0455
www.jacquardproducts.com
Paint, ink, dye, resists, ink-jet fabric

RED PEARL RUBBER STAMPS
Fax: 206-903-8202
www.fredbmullett.com/redpearl/
Intaglio and relief stamps of Chinese calligraphy and seals

GRAFIX
800-447-2349
216-581-9050
www.grafixarts.com
Shrink film

JANE DÁVILA

is a fiber and mixed media artist who began her professional art career as a printmaker. Her work can be found in many private and corporate collections worldwide. She teaches art quilting and surface design nationally and at The Country Quilter in Somers, New York, the store that she and her mother, Claire Oehler, opened in 1990. Jane is a regional representative for Studio Art Quilt Associates. She and her husband, Carlos, an abstract oil painter, live in Ridgefield, Connecticut.

Websites: www.janedavila.com and janedavila.etsy.com
Blog: janedavila.blogspot.com
Email: info@janedavila.com

ELIN WATERSTON

is an award-winning textile and mixed media artist and graphic designer. She has a BA and an MFA in design. Elin is inspired by her favorite artists, known and unknown, and by international folk art. She is the visual arts director, as well as an art instructor, at the Katonah Art Center in Katonah, New York. She is an Art*o*mat participating artist. Her work is in many public and private collections and has been exhibited in numerous galleries and museums. She lives in South Salem, New York, with her husband, David, a cinematographer, and their two Westies.

Websites: www.elinwaterston.com and
willlovelogic.etsy.com
Blog: willlovelogic.blogspot.com
Email: info@elinwaterston.com

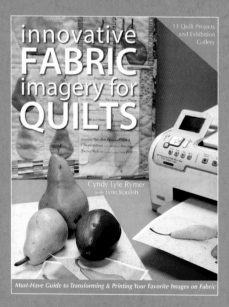
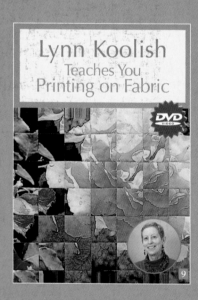